# THE WOMEN'S 1992 VOTING GUIDE

## The Women's Political Action Group

## Edited by Catherine Dee

To American women—and men—who want to
improve the quality of life for everyone.

Created and Packaged by Javnarama
Cover Design by Lenna, Emma, John and Andy
Cover Illustration by Richard Kizu-Blair
Illustrations by Michele Montez

ISBN 1-879682-25-7
First Edition, 1992

Special editions are available at quantity discounts.

For information, please contact:

EarthWorks Press
1400 Shattuck Avenue, Box 25
Berkeley, CA 94709
(510) 652-8533

# ACKNOWLEDGMENTS

*The Women's Political Action Group and Catherine Dee would like to thank everyone who worked to make this book possible, including these individuals and organizations:*

- K Kaufmann
- John Javna
- Ellen Umansky
- Kim Koch
- Brooke Hodess
- Dayna Macy
- Lenna Lebovich
- Fritz Springmeyer
- Lyn Speakman
- Penelope Houston
- Sharilyn Hovind
- Andy Sohn
- Michele Montez
- Jack Mingo
- Sharon Redel
- Richard Kizu-Blair
- Sarah Dee
- Teri Edwards
- Morreen Beetlestone
- Fran Javurek
- Craig Bristol
- Joanne Miller
- John Dollison
- Emma Lauriston
- Denise Silver
- Melanie Foster
- Ruth Mandel
- Janice Steinschneider
- Caroline Eichman
- Betty Murphy
- Susan Faludi
- Center for the American Woman and Politics
- National Women's Political Caucus
- The Fund for the Feminist Majority
- Ms. magazine
- Karen Kraut
- Center for Women's Policy Studies
- Gloria Steinem
- Faye Wattleton
- Susan Sarandon
- Child Care Action Campaign
- Abbe Kaufmann
- Joanne Howes
- Barbara Radford
- Ellen Bravo
- Black Women's Health Project
- Peggy Elath
- Lynn Thompson-Haas
- National Organization for Women
- Estella Cortinas

- Diane Pollock
- Susan Claymon
- Boston Women's Health Book Collective
- National Coalition Against Sexual Assault
- Ellen Galinsky
- Women's Bureau, U.S. Department of Labor
- Planned Parenthood
- National Abortion Rights Action League
- National Abortion Federation
- Alan Guttmacher Institute
- Kelly Jenkins
- National Committee on Pay Equity
- Betsy Hildebrandt
- National Women's Law Center
- Paula Casey
- Pat Groot
- 9 to 5, National Association of Working Women
- Women for Racial and Economic Equality
- Margaret Mann
- Older Women's League
- Becky Rolfe
- San Francisco Women Against Rape
- Wendy Sherman
- National Association for the Education of Young Children
- Maureen Steinbruner
- Marion Banzhaf
- American Cancer Society
- Anne Kasper
- Campaign for Women's Health
- Women's Cancer Resource Center
- Joan Zorza
- Battered Women's Law Project
- Janet Nudelman
- Family Violence Prevention Fund
- Jenny Chung
- National Alliance of Breast Cancer Organizations
- League of Women Voters
- Alyson Reed
- Amanda Smith
- Bill Pierce
- Gretchen Wright
- National Council for Research on Women
- Children's Defense Fund
- Orson Dee
- Joanne Parker
- Mike Litchfield
- Women's Legal Defense Fund
- Irene VonSeydewitz
- Lorrie Bodger
- Mary Hickey
- Kelly Langston
- Y-ME
- The state women's resource group representatives
- Jeff Stafford
- 5th St. Computer

# CONTENTS

# PREFACE

It's hard to believe now, but for the first 144 years of American history, women were not allowed to vote. It wasn't until 1920—after suffragists had struggled for more than 70 years—that the 19th Amendment to the Constitution was passed.

But that didn't automatically give women political power. Most eligible women didn't even register to vote—largely because they still thought politics was an inappropriate interest for the "weaker sex."

This attitude has changed gradually. Every year since 1920, more women have voted. Nonetheless, it wasn't until 1980—just 12 years ago—that an equal number of women and men went to the polls.

That year marked another important milestone in women's voting: Politicians recognized that women's political priorities are often different than men's (the "gender gap") and began changing their positions to accommodate women's viewpoints. Women stopped simply *participating* in the political process...and began *shaping* it.

In 1992, women have more political strength than ever. Fifty-four percent of all registered voters are women, and voting age women outnumber men by *10 million*. Since 1986, women's votes have been the deciding factor in 14 senatorial races and 4 gubernatorial elections.

The opportunity for women voters to make a difference has never been greater. Let's keep the momentum going and use our voting power in November.

—*Representative Patricia Schroeder, D-Colorado,
Representative Olympia Snowe, R-Maine
Co-Chairs, Congressional Caucus for Women's Issues*

# INTRODUCTION

Around election time, you can count on getting a steady stream of "voting guides" from political parties, special interest groups, individual candidates, etc. Unfortunately, they're usually just checklists that recommend candidates. If you want in-depth information about political issues (especially issues that affect women), you've got to do a lot of research on your own...and even then you still may not find what you're looking for.

This is a problem for anyone concerned with women's rights. After all, how can we make issues like pay equity, child support, and sexual harassment part of a mainstream political agenda if people can't even get the basic information needed to understand them?

That's why the Women's Political Action Group has written this book. We believe women will use their political power to protect their rights and improve the quality of their lives if they have access to the facts.

*The Women's 1992 Voting Guide* is not a checklist to take to the polls, and it doesn't endorse parties or candidates. It has one purpose: To provide information, so that you can better understand women's political issues and decide how you want to vote.

This book includes:

• **A clear explanation of eleven key issues.** In each case, we've provided relevant statistics, a political progress report, political goals, and a few thoughts on how to find out if a candidate supports the issue.

• **Congressional voting charts.** We picked 10 bills (5 from the House and 5 from the Senate) that address women's issues—like the Family and Medical Leave Act—and shown how U.S. congressional incumbents voted on each one.

• **Bills currently pending in the U.S. Congress.** A list of legislation that specifically affects women. Call your senators' and representatives' offices to find out how they plan to vote on these bills.

- **Notes on the presidential candidates.** A look at how President Bush and the two leading Democratic contenders (at press time) stand on 5 women's issues.

- **A do-it-yourself local candidate "report card."** A form you can fill out to evaluate local candidates' positions on women's issues.

- **State-by-state legislative summaries.** With the help of local women's groups, we've compiled a list of key "women's bills" currently being addressed in each state legislature. Use this information to evaluate candidates in your area by finding out how they stand on these bills.

- **Names and addresses of local women's groups.** We've listed an organization for each state so you can get more information about local issues and candidates.

- **Election resources.** If you want more specific information on candidates and their records, you can call or write these groups.

## About "Women's Issues"

Some people may ask what makes the issues in this book *women's* issues. After all, issues like child care, pay equity, and family leave are really everyone's concerns.

It's true that these issues do affect everyone—and in a perfect world, they are "people's issues." But currently in our society, these issues directly affect more women's lives than men's. Some issues, like breast cancer and reproductive rights, are obviously more critical to women. Others may not be readily recognized as women's issues...until the statistics are known. For example:

- *Child care* is a women's issue because women are responsible for child care arrangements in more than 90% of American households.

- *Family leave* is a women's issue because two-thirds of the people (not including health care professionals) who take care of the elderly, chronically ill, and disabled are women.

- *Pay equity* is a women's issue because, on average, women still earn only 71¢ for every dollar men earn.

It's important to understand that everyone—not just women—benefits from changes that improve women's lives. Better family leave policies will allow more men to take paternity leave; pay equity policies will benefit families who rely partly or completely on a woman's income; and better enforcement of child support laws will directly benefit children.

As voters, we have the ability to focus attention on these vital issues by questioning candidates, talking to other voters, and ultimately, selecting leaders who will effectively represent our needs. Our votes can help improve women's status, health, careers and home lives.

In the short run, the Women's Political Action Group hopes this information will give women the tools needed to influence 1992 political races—from state legislatures to the presidency. In the long run, however, we hope it will help change the political direction of this country and make the political system more responsive to women's needs.

*—The Women's Political Action Group*
*April 17, 1992*

# WOMEN'S

# ISSUES

# BREAST CANCER

*Every 12 minutes an American woman dies of breast cancer.*

I f you're like most women today, you worry about breast cancer. It's hard not to. The number of cases in the U.S. is increasing dramatically, and while early detection and survival rates are improving slightly, treatment is still traumatic—and not necessarily effective. Worse, there's still no cure in sight.

Researchers say that to find a cure, they must have adequate funding for basic research. But they're not getting it. While breast cancer represents 17% of all cancers diagnosed in the U.S., less than 2% of the funding requested by the National Institutes of Health (the federal health agency) in 1992 is earmarked for breast cancer research.

In the past few years, breast cancer has become a political issue. Last October ("Breast Cancer Awareness Month"), women deluged Congress with 600,000 letters regarding the disease; a national advocacy group called the Breast Cancer Coalition was formed; and grass-roots groups began working all over the country to raise awareness and elect candidates who will support funding for breast cancer research.

## DID YOU KNOW

• In the past decade, the number of American women with breast cancer has risen to epidemic proportions. Since 1980, the figure has increased by 3% each year.

• The American Cancer Society estimates that as many as 1 in 9 women in the U.S. will get breast cancer in their lifetimes. In the 1960s, it was only 1 in 20.

• The breast cancer rate for women in the U.S. is 5 times higher than for women in Asia and Africa.

• In 1990 alone, an estimated 175,000 American women were diagnosed with the disease...and 44,500 died from it.

## PROGRESS REPORT
### Funding for Research

• The National Cancer Institute has not made funding for breast cancer research a high enough priority. For example: A major study of breast cancer and fat in women's diets (believed to be an important risk factor), has been delayed for 10 years due to lack of funding. And many top researchers have left the field for research posts that are better funded.

• However, activists' efforts have begun to have an effect: Congress voted to increase funding for breast cancer research by $42 million for 1992, and a number of bills are being considered to improve early detection and treatment options.

### Mammography

• Until there's a cure for breast cancer and more knowledge about how to prevent it, women have to rely on early detection techniques (mammograms and self-exams). However, studies show that about half of American women over 40 (the age when mammography is recommended) say they have never had a mammogram.

• One of the main reasons women don't have mammograms is the high cost. Thirty nine states require insurance companies to offer some coverage for mammograms, but the full cost isn't usually covered by insurance, Medicare or Medicaid (see p. 28 for details).

• There are over 10,000 mammography machines in the U.S. (compared to 184 machines 10 years ago). However, only about a third of them are in hospitals or breast centers that meet the quality and training standards set by the American College of Radiology.

• The federal government has not set quality standards for mammography centers, and only 9 states have any guidelines.

• The Breast and Cervical Cancer Mortality Prevention Act, allocating funding for states to provide mammograms and Pap smears for low-income women, became law in 1990. However, only 12 states have received money through the act this year.

Some 70% of African American and Latina women have never had a mammogram.

## THE WOMEN'S VOTE: 1992

### 1. Political Goals

• **Increased funding for breast cancer research.** $42 million is a good start, but more funding is desperately needed. Priority area: Research to find the cause of breast cancer and how to prevent it.

• **Better insurance coverage.** Mammograms should be fully covered by health insurance (including Medicaid) for all women age 40 and over.

• **The establishment of nationwide standards for mammography.** Better standards can help ensure that a higher percentage of mammograms are accurate.

• **Universal access to screening and treatment.** All women should have access to quality early detection tests and treatment.

### 2. What to Look For

• Although millions of women are concerned about breast cancer, you're not likely to hear political candidates discussing it. So you may have to do some research on your own.

• If the candidate you're interested in is an incumbent, check our congressional scorecard section (starting on p. 52) to find out how he or she voted on the NIH Revitalization Act, which authorizes breast cancer research, and the Labor-HHS Conference Report, which designates funding for breast cancer research.

• Another tip: "Although men or women candidates may support breast cancer research," says one activist, "women candidates may be more likely to realize the severity of the issue because it affects them personally. As the American Cancer Society has stated, 'Every woman is at risk.' "

### FOR MORE INFORMATION

• **Breast Cancer Action,** P.O. Box 460185, San Francisco, CA 94146. (415) 922-8279. *Call or write for their bimonthly newsletter, which includes action updates on bills before Congress.*

• **Breast Cancer Coalition,** c/o National Alliance of Breast Cancer Organizations, Attn: Amy Langer, 1180 Avenue of the Americas, Second Floor, New York, NY 10036. (800) 221-2141. *An organization of more than 140 groups that supports legislative efforts to increase funding for breast cancer.*

About 80% of women in one poll said they'd best be represented by women congress members.

# CHILD CARE

*According to recent polls, 84% of Americans believe in providing quality child care to all children, regardless of their parents' ability to pay.*

I
f you're a working mother with small children, you know that suitable day care is critical to their well-being...and to your peace of mind.

Finding good day care has never been an easy task—but now, with so many women working, it's even more difficult. The number of quality day care facilities has not grown fast enough to keep up with the increasing demand. As a result, many women have to settle for whatever's available—shuffling the kids around between family, friends, and private centers—and just hope it all works out.

Ideally, this should be a family issue, not just a women's issue. However, in the U.S., women have traditionally been responsible for arranging and overseeing child care. In fact, according to the Child Care Action Campaign, women make the child care arrangements in more than 90% of American households.

If current employment trends continue, two-thirds of all school-age children will have mothers in the work force by 1995. It's time to make child care a national priority.

## DID YOU KNOW

• More than 50% of all American mothers with infants age one or under are either employed or looking for work.

• For many single mothers, the availability of affordable child care can be the difference between welfare and work. A survey of mothers on welfare in Washington State found that two-thirds were unable to work due to a lack of affordable child care.

• About 36 million children age 14 and under have working mothers. But licensed child care facilities in the United States only have the capacity to care for 5.2 million children. That means the parents of more than 30 million children have to find other solutions.

• An estimated 3.5 million "latchkey kids," children ages 6-13,

More women have been elected to the U.S. Congress from New York than from any other state go home to empty houses every afternoon.

• Although financial advisors generally recommend spending no more than 10% of family income on child care, low-income families typically have to spend 20-26% of their incomes.

• Recent national polls show that two-thirds of day care centers have waiting lists, and one-third of U.S. parents feel that the child care they *can* afford is probably not of high quality.

## PROGRESS REPORT

No one—least of all the federal government—has been willing to take responsibility for providing leadership coordinating child care policy. The result has been a combination of successes and failures.

### Funding

• Child care has been one of the major casualties of the budget crunch of the last decade. Under the Reagan administration, federal funding for child care was cut in half. Today it remains below 1981 levels—even though there are now about 12% more mothers in the work force with children under age 6.

• The result: In the last ten years, only 20 states have increased funding for and expanded child care programs, while 23 have reduced the number of children they can serve. According to the Center for Policy Alternatives, for instance, in 1990, North Carolina had a waiting list of 10,000 for places in its government-subsidized day care programs.

• The good news: In 1990, Congress passed two bills authorizing increased spending for child care. If fully funded over the next five years, these new programs will pump more than $2 billion into increasing the supply of affordable, quality child care, and providing subsidies for low-income families.

### Regulations

• There are still no federal minimum health and safety requirements for child care providers. The result: Twenty-five states don't even have regulations limiting the number of children who can attend a center at one time.

• In addition, an estimated 80-90% of the nation's 1.75 million home-based child care providers are unlicensed and unregulated.

**An estimated 45% of women legislators think of themselves as feminists.**

In fact, half of the states have no minimum education or training requirements for people hired to be child care workers.

### Compensation

• A recent survey of child care providers found that salaries in the field have remained virtually unchanged for 15 years. Child care workers, 98% of whom are women, generally make less than parking lot attendants. Their average wage is about $7.50 an hour.

• The result: A high staff turnover rate that compromises consistency and quality of care. An estimated 40-60% of child care workers leave their jobs each year.

### Employer-Funded Child Care

• Today only about 5,600 businesses in the U.S. provide their employees with some kind of support for child care. About 1,400 have established child care centers on or near their work sites.

• But a growing number of American employers are finding out that helping working parents with child care makes good business sense. Studies show that offering child care benefits not only reduces employee absenteeism and turnover but also boosts productivity and morale.

## THE WOMEN'S VOTE: 1992

### 1. Political Goals

• **Increased funding for child care programs.** The new funding passed by Congress is only the first step. In the next few years, federal and state funding initiatives will be needed to expand the number and quality of child care programs, raise salaries of child care workers, and help low-income families pay for child care.

• **A national child care office.** Eighty-seven percent of Americans believe the responsibility for child care should be shared by businesses and federal, state and local governments. Experts say a national office could provide the necessary leadership and policy coordination.

• **Minimum health and safety standards for day care centers and home-based providers.** While some states have adequate health and safety regulations, nationwide standards are needed to ensure quality care.

The number of U.S. firms that offer child care benefits has increased almost 17 times since 1978.

• **Business incentives.** Businesses that provide child care benefits should be rewarded with tax credits or other incentives. Local lawmakers can also pass zoning laws that will encourage many builders and new businesses to include space for child care facilities.

### 2. What to Look For

• Check a candidate's campaign literature. In 1992, child care is considered a major issue—so if someone supports increased child care funding, there's a good chance they'll say so.

• If there's no specific mention of child care, check out the candidate's stand on education. "See what aspects of education they're interested in," suggests Caroline Eichman of the Child Care Action Campaign. "If early childhood education is a priority, they probably support child care issues."

• Caution: If a candidate talks about being "pro-family," take a closer look at her or his positions. Often this political buzzword means the candidate believes that women shouldn't be in the work force at all, but at home taking care of the kids...They may consider women who don't stay home bad mothers. "Guilt is a big factor in the rhetoric against child care," says Eichman. "But most working women don't have the option of staying home with the kids, even if they want to. For the bulk of American families, child care is an economic necessity."

### FOR MORE INFORMATION

• **Child Care Action Campaign,** 330 Seventh Ave., 17th Floor, New York, NY 10001. (212) 239-0138. *Write for their free fact sheets.*

Some 25% of mothers who stay home say they'd go to work if affordable child care were available.

# CHILD SUPPORT

*In 1989, the average child support a woman received was $2,995 per year. That's less than a quarter of the average annual cost of raising a child.*

Today American couples getting married for the first time have a 60% chance of getting divorced...and half of *all* U.S. marriages end in divorce.

Because mothers usually retain custody of children when a marriage ends, child support is an important issue for women—not just as a matter of fairness (i.e., sharing the financial burden of raising children equally), but as a matter of survival.

For example, if you're a single divorced mother, child support payments may be the difference between barely scraping by and being able to provide a decent standard of living for yourself and your children. Yet, according to one study, as many as 2/3 of divorced fathers fail to make their payments.

Many judges and politicians consider child support a domestic issue. But it's really an issue of economic child abuse. We need to elect candidates who understand this...and are willing to make child support enforcement a higher priority.

**DID YOU KNOW**

• Divorce is one of the leading causes of poverty among women and children. In 1990, about a third of divorced and separated women with children under 21 were living below the poverty level.

• In the first year after a divorce, a wife's income drops an average of 30%, while a husband's rises 10-15% (compared to the income they had while they were married).

• This makes child support more crucial to America's children, who are more likely to remain with their mothers. But according to the Office of Child Support Enforcement, in 1989, more than *$18 billion* in current and prior year child support went unpaid.

• Two-thirds of men questioned in a study in Denver, Colorado, had smaller monthly child support payments than car payments. However, more than half of the men were behind on their child

The first woman in the U.S. House of Representatives was Jeannette Rankin (R-MT), in 1917.

support payments, but almost all had their cars paid up.

• Some experts estimate that new federal child support legislation will decrease the number of women and children living in poverty by 25-40%.

## PROGRESS REPORT
### The Bad News

• In 1975, the Social Security Act established the Child Support Program as a separate unit in the Department of Health and Human Services. Since then, the government has given the program lower and lower priority; in fact, the unit has been merged with other departments twice.

• In 1988, a federal audit found that 35 states weren't complying with federal child support laws. In response, Congress passed the Family Support Act of 1988 to strengthen previous child support legislation. However, the Federal Office of Child Support Enforcement has been slow to come up with regulations to make enforcement possible.

• Currently in most states (34), a parent has to go to court in order to collect unpaid child support. The result: Courts are overburdened with these cases—despite the fact that paperwork for automatic deductions could be handled by "administrative process" in each state's child support office instead.

### The Good News

• New state laws are beginning to provide some relief. In Washington State, for example, when new employees fill out W-4 forms, they must answer the question, "Do you have a child support obligation?" This makes it easier to track down non-paying parents and/or deduct the money from their paychecks.

• In some states, child support payments are now being determined objectively, based on the divorcing couple's income. In Wisconsin, payments are based on a flat percentage of the non-custodial parent's income.

• Automatic deduction of child support will be standard nationwide by 1994. And by 1995, all child support records should be automated to decrease the time it takes to track down non-paying parents.

After the Thomas hearings, direct mail contributions to women's groups increased 30-50%.

- There is also a bill in Congress called the Child Support Enforcement Improvements Act. Its provisions include enforcing court orders requiring non-custodial parents to pay for children's medical expenses.

## THE WOMEN'S VOTE: 1992

### 1. Political Goals

- **Stronger child support laws.** Laws should be re-evaluated and structured to ensure that women and children depending on child support have a decent standard of living.

- **The adoption of "administrative process" by states.** If states are required to process paperwork out of court, child support enforcement will be more efficient and create less of a burden for courts.

- **The establishment of state child support advisory committees.** We need to elect officials willing to establish these groups, which would include representatives from all sectors that deal with child support (judges, clerks, social workers, parents, etc.). Joint decision-making would help the system run more smoothly, and child support laws would more likely be enforced.

### 2. What to Look For

- Child support isn't likely to be any candidate's high-priority political issue this year. But you can probably tell how candidates stand on child support by finding out how they feel about other issues related to children.

- According to Betty Murphy of the National Child Support Advocacy Coalition, "If issues like education and child care aren't front and center on their agenda, chances are they view child support as just a civil matter—a domestic issue," she says. "You can't be *for* kids and *against* stronger child support laws."

## FOR MORE INFORMATION

- **National Child Support Advocacy Coalition (NCSAC)**, P.O. Box 420, Hendersonville, TN 37077. *Lobbies for better child support enforcement. For information, send $5 and a self-addressed, stamped (58¢) envelope.*

- **National Women's Law Center**, 1616 P St. NW, Suite 100, Washington, D.C. 20036. (202) 328-5160. *Free publications on child support.*

New Hampshire has the highest percentage of women county board members of any state.

# DOMESTIC VIOLENCE

*A woman in the U.S. is more likely to be assaulted, injured, raped or killed by a male partner than by any other assailant.*

Domestic violence is a much more serious problem than most people realize: Three to four million women are battered by their husbands or partners in the U.S. each year.

And although the solution may seem obvious—just end the relationship and walk away—it really isn't that easy. Battered women often have no money and nowhere to go to escape an abusive partner. They may also be too scared; their partners may have threatened more violence if they leave. Battered women may have even called the police or gone to court to get a restraining order...and been beaten again.

Studies show that, unfortunately, police officers seldom arrest men who physically abuse their partners, even if there's clear evidence of their guilt. Officers are usually trained to simply mediate—to get both parties "calmed down."

This slap-on-the-wrist approach to domestic violence is inappropriate. There are many things we can do to make the system work for battered women—starting with electing candidates who really care about helping them.

## DID YOU KNOW

• Twenty percent of female emergency room patients are battered women.

• A third of all homeless women and children in the U.S. are fleeing domestic violence.

• Only 50% of U.S. cities and counties have crisis telephone hotlines, legal advocacy, and shelters for battered women and their children.

• Existing battered women's shelters are overcrowded and underfunded. An estimated 250,000 women and children (40% of those seeking shelter) are turned away every year.

• Thirty percent of female homicide victims are killed by their male partners.

The first U.S. shelter for battered women opened in a private home in 1964.

## PROGRESS REPORT

### The Bad News

• The federal government has not provided much support for battered women's shelters, law enforcement training or prevention. In the 1980s, less than $50 million a year was designated for these services.

• Only fifteen states have made it mandatory to arrest batterers when there is "probable cause" (evidence like bruises, torn clothing, or broken furniture) that a crime has occurred. In other states, arrest is encouraged but not required, which doesn't do much good. In Texas, for example, a law encouraging probable cause arrest did not increase domestic violence arrests and convictions.

• Although stalking (following and harassing victims) is common, state laws on restraining orders for offenders have been unevenly applied and enforced. Only 24 states require police officers to arrest men who violate the orders in domestic violence cases. And while almost all states allow judges to protect women by temporarily evicting abusive partners, few judges do.

### The Good News

• Traditionally, domestic violence laws have applied only to married couples. Legislation is being introduced in some states (e.g., Kentucky and Vermont) to expand the definition of domestic violence to include people who live (or have lived) together.

• A small number of courts are being adapted to meet the needs of battered women. An all-night court in Philadelphia, Pennsylvania—the first of its kind in the nation—makes it easier for battered women to get emergency restraining orders.

• In Baltimore, Maryland, all new judges are required to take a one-day course on domestic violence issues.

• Some states (e.g., Florida and New Jersey) are introducing legislation to criminalize stalking.

• A bill in Congress—the Violence Against Women Act—would provide $300 million for shelters and the training of police, prosecutors and judges to handle domestic violence cases. It would also establish a ommission on Violent Crimes Against Women.

In 1990, 59% of women candidates won their races in state legislative elections.

## THE WOMEN'S VOTE: 1992

### 1. Political Goals

• **Passage of the Violence Against Women Act.** Women victimized because of their gender deserve the same civil rights protection that now exists for victims attacked because of their race, ethnic background or sexual orientation.

• **Mandatory arrest laws for batterers.** New laws can make a difference. In 1984, Washington State passed a law requiring police to arrest batterers. The result: Arrests jumped 400% and convictions increased 300%.

• **Enforcement of domestic violence laws.** Police officers, prosecutors and judges should receive special training on domestic violence laws and their enforcement. Training requirements should be written into state domestic violence laws and local policies.

• **More shelters and services for battered women.** Every city and county should have crisis lines, legal advocacy and shelters.

### 2. What to Look For

• Domestic violence isn't likely to be a topic of discussion for most candidates. So if you're interested in someone's position on the issue, you'll probably have to ask.

• If they answer you with phrases like "preserving the family unit" and "family values," they may not take domestic violence seriously enough. These terms often indicate a person believes that preserving a marriage is more important than protecting a woman.

• If a candidate says he or she believes in "decriminalization" or "diversion" of batterers to alcohol/drug rehabilitation programs, take a closer look. According to Janet Nudelman of the Family Violence Prevention Fund, "Sometimes diversion is the right solution, but it's inappropriate when there is a serious injury or a weapon is involved, or when it's an attempted homicide."

### FOR MORE INFORMATION

• **Family Violence Prevention Fund,** Building One, Suite 200, 1001 Potrero Avenue, San Francisco, CA 94110. (415) 821-4553. *Extensive information (most of it free) on domestic violence legislation at the state and federal levels.*

A woman of color has never been elected to the U.S. Senate.

# FAMILY LEAVE

*The U.S. is the only industrialized country without
a national family leave policy.*

What would you do if your child were sick and needed your attention for a couple of weeks? Would your employer give you the time off? Would you be worried about getting fired if you took too much time?

Family leave (paid or unpaid time off to care for children or aging parents) is a common job benefit in the rest of the world, but not in the U.S. We have no national family leave policy, and fewer than 16% of the companies in the *Fortune 1,000* have set up their own leave policies.

Why is this a women's issue? Family responsibilities are still largely considered "women's work," even though the majority of women now work outside the home. For example, two-thirds of the people (not including health care professionals) who take care of America's elderly, chronically ill and disabled are women.

Women who take responsibility for their families are performing an essential service for society. We should support them by electing politicians who will push for a national family leave policy.

**DID YOU KNOW**

• In the U.S., half of all mothers with children ages 1 or younger, and 75% of mothers with children aged 6-17, work outside the home.

• Most women work because of economic necessity. A 1990 study at Columbia University found that children in two-parent families in which only one parent works are 10 times more likely to live in poverty than children in two-parent families in which both parents work.

• According to the Institute for Women's Policy Research, working families lose more than $600 million in earnings each year because they can't take family leave. Government programs to assist these families cost U.S. taxpayers an estimated $108 million a year.

• According to a 1990 study, 11-13% of working women caring for their aging parents are forced to leave work so they can provide care.

Today 69% of women aged 18-64 work, compared to 33% in 1950.

- A survey by the Small Business Association showed that the cost to an employer of permanently replacing a worker is significantly higher than the cost of granting a leave.

- According to a recent Gallup poll, 81% of Americans support legislation for unpaid family and medical leave.

## PROGRESS REPORT

### Legislation

- In theory, the Pregnancy Disability Act of 1978 protects pregnant women and new mothers from job discrimination or dismissal. But only 40% of U.S. employers have maternity leave policies.

- Women are still sometimes demoted, transferred, forced to quit or fired when they are pregnant or after having their babies. In 1990, the Equal Employment Opportunity Commission received more than 2,800 complaints of pregnancy discrimination.

- Since 1986, repeated efforts to pass a national family and medical leave bill have failed. President Bush vetoed the 1990 Family and Medical Leave Act. A new version introduced in Congress in 1991 would require businesses with 50 or more workers to provide employees with up to 12 weeks of unpaid, job-protected leave...but President Bush has threatened another veto. Individual states are going ahead and passing their own family leave laws (at last count, 18 states had laws).

### The Private Sector

- Many employers believe family leave is impractical and expensive—they think it interferes with productivity. However, studies show that leave policies can *improve* profitability at big companies. In one nationwide survey of employers with leave policies, 49% reported improved productivity and 65% reduced employee turnover as a result. Some experts estimate that it costs employers 3-5 times more to replace an employee than to cover his or her leave.

- According to Women for Racial & Economic Equality (WREE), The Family and Medical Leave Act would cost all U.S. businesses a combined total of $188 million a year. That's less than 1/2 of 1% of total company profits—about $4.50 per employee.

- Some large companies have discovered the benefits of adopting family leave policies. At Merck, a pharmaceutical company, new

1991 was the first year that at least one woman served in each state legislature.

parents can take up to 6 months of leave with partial pay and benefits. IBM offers employees job-guaranteed leaves of up to 3 years.

• Family leave policies are not always cost-effective for businesses with fewer than 50 employees. Experts say the solution is to provide subsidies and tax credits to small businesses as incentives for adopting leave policies. However, some states (e.g., Oregon and Vermont) are trying to pass laws making family leave available for employees at smaller companies.

## THE WOMEN'S VOTE: 1992

### 1. Political Goals

• **Passage of the Family and Medical Leave Act.** Laws should guarantee employees unpaid, job-protected leave of at least 12 weeks—with benefits—to care for newborns and newly adopted children, seriously ill family members, or for the employee to attend to his or her own personal illness.

• **Government subsidies and tax credits for small companies that grant leave.** About 40% of working women are employed by small businesses that are routinely exempted from state family leave laws.

### 2. What to Look For

• If the candidates you're interested in are congressional incumbents, see how they voted on the 1991 version of the Family and Medical Leave Act (see the scorecard section beginning on p. 52).

• According to Ellen Galinsky of the Families and Work Institute, voters should be cautious about candidates who say they support only voluntary measures to encourage businesses to adopt family leave policies. Simply suggesting that businesses institute leave policies isn't likely to spark major changes.

• If there's no direct indication of how a candidate stands on this issue, take a look at her or his stand on related issues like child care and long-term health coverage for the elderly. Someone who supports quality care for all members of the family is likely to support family leave, too.

## FOR MORE INFORMATION

• **Families and Work Institute,** 330 7th Ave., New York, NY 10001. (212) 465-2044. *A center for policy and research on work and family life and a clearinghouse for information on family leave.*

The number of women in state legislatures has more than quadrupled since 1969.

# HEALTH CARE

*Fifteen million American women don't have health insurance.*

Health care is a major issue of the 1992 election campaign. As medical costs rise and insurance companies and employers cut back, access to basic health care is becoming more and more difficult.

Of course, the current health care crisis affects both men and women. But women are more at risk for several reasons: They use health care services an estimated 30% more than men (because they need services like mammograms and prenatal care); only about half of all women working full time are insured by their employers; and even if women have *some* coverage, they're more likely to be underinsured for basic health care needs.

Health care is already a political issue; now we need to let candidates know how important it is as a *women's* issue.

## DID YOU KNOW

• 55% of women work in clerical, sales or service jobs, which are less likely to be covered by employer-paid group insurance plans.

• Part-time workers—two-thirds of whom are women—rarely have employer-paid health insurance.

• More than 70% of working single mothers do not have employer-paid health insurance that also covers their children.

• Divorced women are half as likely as married women to have insurance (many married women are covered under their husbands' plans).

• Inadequate coverage for prenatal care has contributed to saddling the U.S. with one of the highest infant mortality rates among industrialized countries. We currently rank 20 of 21—only South Africa is higher.

• Insurance companies have traditionally based their coverage policies on the needs of adult males. As a result, some basic health care needs that apply only to women are viewed as "extras," and are therefore less likely to be covered.

Women over 65 must often pay as much as 25% of their income for out-of-pocket medical expenses.

• Older women are particularly hard hit by poor insurance coverage. Women are more likely to need long-term care than men because they tend to live longer (at age 75, women outnumber men 2 to 1). However, private insurance and Medicare don't adequately cover long-term care. And a recent study found that while Medicaid paid almost half of the health care expenses of men over 65, it paid only a third for women over 65.

• Health insurance coverage for mammograms is inadequate for most women. Although doctors recommend baseline mammograms for all women beginning at age 40, Blue Cross-Blue Shield pays for mammograms only after age 50. The problem is worse for women who rely on Medicare or Medicaid. The average cost of a mammogram is $104, but the maximum Medicare reimbursement is $55. Many states pay even less (e.g., New York pays $30 and Pennsylvania $6 per mammogram).

## PROGRESS REPORT

• Lawmakers are attempting to address the health insurance crisis. Since 1990, numerous health care reform bills have been introduced in Congress. Some require employers to pay into a national health care fund or provide insurance for workers (the "pay or play" plans). Others would establish a national health care system with varying levels of guaranteed coverage.

• In 1990, the Congressional Caucus for Women's Issues introduced the Women's Health Equity Act, a package of bills including legislation to increase funding for women's health services. Portions of the bill were pulled and included in the National Institutes of Health (NIH) Revitalization Act, which was passed by both the House of Representatives and the Senate.

• The NIH bill authorizes funds for research on breast, ovarian, and cervical cancers, osteoporosis, and contraceptive and infertility research centers. It would permanently establish an Office of Research on Women's Health at NIH. However, President Bush has threatened to veto this legislation because it has a provision that would lift the ban on research using fetal tissue.

## THE WOMEN'S VOTE: 1992
### 1. Political Goals
Insurance coverage for all women's health care needs,

**regardless of age, marital status or job status.** Women's health care services should be covered by both private and public insurance plans. A national health care plan may be necessary to accomplish this.

## 2. What to Look For
• According to Anne Kasper of the Campaign for Women's Health, "With health insurance a hot campaign issue, the first thing to do is see whether a candidate has drafted his or her own health care reform proposal. If not, see which one of the current reform proposals he or she is supporting."
• Check to see if the plan specifically covers mammograms, prenatal and maternal care, Pap smears, prenatal care, long-term care for older women, and family planning services.
• "Most candidates will say they are for reform," Kasper says. "But if you look at the plans they've drafted, they only tinker with the current system or offer partial solutions...so make sure the candidate is backing a plan that would meet all women's health insurance needs."

## FOR MORE INFORMATION
• **Campaign for Women's Health,** 666 Eleventh St. NW, Washington, D.C. 20001. (202) 783-6686. *A coalition of more than 60 organizations working at the state and federal levels. Send a self-addressed, stamped 8 1/2 x 11" envelope for their free brochure on women and health care reform. Also available: Analyses of specific health care reform bills.*

Women currently hold 18% of the seats in state legislatures.

# MEDICAL RESEARCH

*Although heart disease is the #1 killer of women, most major studies of heart disease have not included women subjects.*

If you take prescription drugs or buy over-the-counter drugs, you've probably always assumed that the dosages—and any potential side effects—have been studied in both women and men.

That's not necessarily the case. Believe it or not, the dosages of most medicines are determined in studies that include men subjects only...even if women are more likely to get the disease or take the drug being studied. For example, 90% of all diet pills are taken by women, but the active ingredient, *phenylpropanolamine*, has only been tested on men.

Doctors say women are excluded from drug trials and other medical testing because their monthly hormonal changes may affect the outcome of tightly controlled studies. But it is precisely *because* of these hormonal changes that women need to be included. (Even studies on the problems of older people—when women's hormones are no longer an issue—have excluded women.)

This inequity in research translates into lower quality medical care for women. Since research on women's health isn't given a high priority, there is a gap in medical research; doctors know less about women than they should.

The government is constantly spending money on medical research. The people we elect should make sure more of it is spent on women's health.

## DID YOU KNOW

• A major study on the use of aspirin to prevent heart attacks was done with more than 22,000 male subjects and no females. In addition, the National Institutes of Health (the federal health research agency) studied lifestyle factors related to heart disease using almost 13,000 men and no women subjects.

• An estimated 12,000 women died from ovarian cancer in 1991. But scientists at the National Institutes of Health (NIH) have not

In 1987, a researcher at Rockefeller University did a study on the effects requested funds to develop an effective screening test (like mammography for breast cancer). The result: In 70% of women diagnosed with ovarian cancer, the disease is already in its advanced stages.

• In the U.S., women are the fastest growing group of people with AIDS. But symptoms that could signal AIDS that are found only in women—like yeast infections and cervical cancer—are not included in the government's official diagnosis of the disease. One result: Women with AIDS are diagnosed later and die an estimated 3-5 times faster than men.

• Studies have shown that when women and men go to a doctor with the same symptoms, men are more likely to receive a physical examination or tests, while women are more likely to be sent home with a prescription for drugs or tranquilizers.

## PROGRESS REPORT
### The National Institutes of Health

• In 1986, the NIH published new guidelines requiring all government-funded research to include women. Three years later, at the request of the Congressional Caucus for Women's Issues, the General Accounting Office (GAO) found that the guidelines were not being enforced and women were still being excluded from major studies.

• In 1990, in response to the GAO study, the NIH established an Office of Research on Women's Health to monitor compliance with NIH guidelines and ensure that all government-funded research projects include women. The Office also funds research to fill the gaps created by the exclusion of women from medical research.

• In 1991, the NIH got its first female director, Dr. Bernadine Healy. She's planning a $500 million long-term study on women's health, and setting up an office of gynecology and obstetrics.

### The Women's Health Equity Act
• Following the GAO report, the Congressional Caucus for Women's Issues introduced the Women's Health Equity Act, a package of bills that would provide over $237 million in increased funding for women's health research and set guidelines for

of a high-fat diet on breast cancer...using only male subjects.

including women in government-funded research.

• Sections of the act were passed by the House in 1991 as part of a bill called the NIH Revitalization Act. If passed by the Senate this year, the bill will increase funding for women's health research by $90 million and require that women be included in clinical drug trials. But President Bush has pledged to veto it because it contains an amendment lifting the ban on research involving fetal tissue.

## THE WOMEN'S VOTE: 1992

### 1. Political Goals

• **More funding for women's health research.** More money is urgently needed to study breast and ovarian cancers, osteoporosis and menopause.

• **New research guidelines that include women.** Excluding women from medical research and drug trials has kept doctors in the dark about many aspects of women's health. Congress should enact strong guidelines and make sure they're rigorously enforced.

### 2. What to Look For

• You're not likely to hear candidates talking about medical research for women this year...unless you ask them about it.

• If you do bring it up, here's something to consider: "Candidates may say they support women's health research but they can't vote for certain appropriations bills because of controversial amendments" (e.g., lifting the gag rule on family planning clinics), says Joanne Howes of the Society for the Advancement of Women's Health Research. "We say it's a matter of priorities. If you're really for women's health research, you'll vote for the bills."

• If the candidate you're considering is an incumbent, check the congressional scorecard section beginning on p. 52. See how members of Congress voted on the Labor-HHS Conference Report, and how Representatives voted on the NIH Revitalization Act.

### FOR MORE INFORMATION

• **Society for the Advancement of Women's Health Research,** 1601 Connecticut Ave., NW, Suite 801, Washington, D.C. 20009. (202) 328-2200. *A research and advocacy group dealing with women's health issues.*

First woman in the U.S. Senate: Rebecca Latimer Felton (D-GA) in 1922.

# PAY EQUITY

*The average weekly wage for American women is $315; for men, it's $449.*

The Equal Pay Act—passed in 1963—was supposed to guarantee that people who do the same or similar work are paid the same salary.

But if you're a working woman, there's still a good chance your male colleagues make more money than you...even if you have the same job description, have been with the company longer and have more experience. According to the National Committee on Pay Equity, American women still earn only an average of about 71 cents for every dollar men earn.

Why is the wage discrepancy so large?

Some people say it's because women don't get the same level of professional education as men, make less challenging career choices, and take more time off for raising children (and other family responsibilities). And to some extent, they're right. But statistics show that 25-50% of the difference in women's and men's wages has nothing to do with *any* of these factors. As one expert puts it, "Basically, the earnings gap is discrimination, pure and simple, based on the old sexist idea that women's work is worth less than men's."

It's time we elected politicians who are truly committed to eliminating the earnings gap.

## DID YOU KNOW

• Pay equity isn't just an issue of fairness; 86% of employed women work in order to support themselves or their families—they need the income just as much as men do.

• Women earn less than men at every level. According to a 1990 *Business Week* survey, even entry-level jobs for female business school graduates paid 12% less than entry-level jobs for male grads.

• Over half of all women work in low-paying clerical, retail sales or service jobs. Only 10% of women workers earn more than $12.66 hourly.

• Studies show that the more women there are in a given job category, the lower the pay.

**Minnesota was the first state to legislate and implement pay equity in public employment.**

• Even men in female-dominated fields earn more than women. For example, male nurses earn an average of 10% more than female nurses.

• The wage gap is even wider for women of color—on the average, for every dollar men earn, African American women earn 62 cents and Latina women earn 54 cents.

## PROGRESS REPORT

### The Good News

• A growing number of city and state governments are adopting pay equity policies for their employees. As of 1992, 20 states had either begun or completed raising the salaries of women and minorities to achieve pay equity. Another 17 states had initiated research on their wage-setting policies.

• Over the past decade, pay equity raises made by state and local governments have added over $450 million to workers' paychecks.

• Salary increases for pay equity have not overinflated payrolls as many businesses predicted. Pay equity raises have added an average of only 2-5% to payrolls. In Minnesota, where a statewide pay equity program has been implemented, raises phased in over a 4-year period cost less than 1% per year.

• Some labor unions have successfully negotiated wage increases to compensate for past wage discrimination. For example, a union in Washington State negotiated a collective bargaining agreement to pay a total of $100 million to state employees over a period of time.

### The Bad News

• Although the Equal Pay Act has been a U.S. law since 1963, federal support for pay equity has been less than enthusiastic. The Equal Employment Opportunity Commission (EEOC) filed only 7 Equal Pay Act cases in federal court in 1989, and only 8 in 1990. And the last time federal wage-setting policies were revised was in 1923!

• However, in March 1989, Congress ordered the General Accounting Office to conduct a preliminary study of sex- and race-based wage discrimination in the federal work force. The study was finally begun in the fall of 1991; the final report is expected in January 1993.

The first equal pay bill was introduced in Congress in 1943.

• The Pay Equity Technical Assistance Act, which would establish a clearinghouse in the Department of Labor to provide information on pay equity, came up as part of other legislation in the 102st Congress—but ultimately was rejected.

## THE WOMEN'S VOTE: 1992

### 1. Political Goals

• **Better enforcement of the Equal Pay Act.** Elected officials need to put pressure on the EEOC to increase the number of wage discrimination cases it prosecutes each year.

• **More state and local pay equity policies.** More laws are needed to ensure that pay equity policies are adopted by state and local governments and private businesses. Currently, only one state—Minnesota—has a law requiring pay equity for all state and local employees. No states have pay equity laws for private businesses.

• **Passage of the Pay Equity Technical Assistance Act.** Rejected as part of the new Civil Rights Act, it should be reintroduced and passed.

### 2. What to Look For

• No federal legislation on pay equity is pending right now. However, polls show strong voter support for it, so candidates may make it a campaign issue. Check their campaign literature.

• Another test: Find out if the candidate supports requiring equal pay for workers with similar skills, responsibilities, and education—even if the jobs are different.

• Some candidates argue that pay equity is "anti-business," claiming it will overinflate U.S. payrolls. This may sound reasonable, especially when people are worried about the economy, but the Minnesota law has already proven that hypothesis incorrect.

### FOR MORE INFORMATION

• **National Committee on Pay Equity,** 1126 16th St. NW, Suite 411, Washington, D.C. 20036. (202) 331-7343. *A national coalition working to achieve pay equity. Write for their publications list.*

# RAPE

*It's estimated that only .03% of all rapes result in prison terms.*

The United States has the highest incidence of rape of all Western nations. According to the FBI, a woman reports a rape approximately every six minutes...and that's only part of the story. Despite new laws and programs that encourage victims to report the crime, an estimated 90% of all rapes are still unreported.

Women hesitate to speak up for several reasons: Rape victims are still blamed for having "asked for it" (by wearing provocative clothing, etc.); a rape victim's character and sexual background are almost always questioned in court; and many district attorneys are reluctant to prosecute rapists unless there is corroborating physical evidence—e.g., cuts, bruises, torn clothes.

Since the establishment of the first rape crisis centers 20 years ago, knowledge about rape has improved dramatically. For example, rape is no longer defined as "sexual assault by a stranger"; we now know that in as many as 85% of all rapes, the victim knows her assailant (referred to as "acquaintance" or "date" rape).

This year, let's make the fight to prevent rape, and to protect the rights of rape victims, a political issue.

## DID YOU KNOW

• According to a report by the Senate Judiciary Committee, women in the U.S. are eight times more likely to be raped than women in Europe, and 20 times more likely than women in Japan.

• Rape is a crime of violence, not spur-of-the-moment passion. An estimated 91% of sexual assaults are actually planned by the assailant.

• Nationwide, there are only about 600 rape crisis centers.

• In 90% of rapes in the U.S., both the victim and assailant are from the same ethnic or racial background.

• Misconceptions about rape begin early: In a recent study of middle school students, 1/4 of the boys and 1/6 of the girls said it

**Fewer than half of all states pay for abortions for women pregnant through rape or incest.**

was acceptable for a man to force a woman to have sex with him if he had spent money on her (e.g., entertaining her, buying her gifts).

## PROGRESS REPORT

• In the mid-1970s, a National Center for the Prevention and Control of Rape was established to fund research and offer training to people who work with rape victims. However, during the Reagan administration it was absorbed by the National Institutes of Mental Health.

• Most rape crisis centers rely on a combination of federal, state and private funds. But funding losses due to government cuts and the recession have hit them hard. (North Dakota, for example, lost all of its federal matching funds for rape prevention services in 1990.) The result: Rape victims who can't afford private therapy may wait weeks or months to get counseling at a local rape crisis center.

• Rape legislation reforms depend on state, rather than national, elections. Each state determines its own criminal definition of rape, sets sentences for offenders and conditions for their release, and can allocate funding for rape crisis centers and rape prevention education programs.

• State laws can also require police and other criminal justice personnel to get special training for handling rape cases. Currently a few states (e.g., California and Nevada) require police officers, district attorneys and judges to get some training teaching them about rape victims' needs. This helps them understand the victim's perspective.

• There is currently a bill in Congress called The Violence Against Women Act. It would authorize $65-$70 million for rape prevention and education, $300 million for law enforcement efforts to combat sex crimes, and $20 million for college rape prevention and education programs. The bill was stalled in the Senate at press time.

• Another bill pending in Congress, the Higher Education Act, would authorize funds for campus rape education and prevention workshops.

The fastest-growing group in American electoral politics: African American women.

## THE WOMEN'S VOTE: 1992

### 1. Political Goals

• **Passage of the Violence Against Women Act.** More money is needed to enforce laws, train people who work with rape victims, and pay for rape prevention education.

• **Adequate funding for rape crisis centers.** This is a priority. More rape victims are being urged to seek counseling at the same time that funding for counseling is being cut.

• **Required training for police officers and district attorneys.** It's important for people handling rape cases to understand the needs of rape victims.

### 2. What to Look For

• "Typically, sexual assault does not become a campaign issue," says Pat Groot of the National Network for Victims of Sexual Assault. "I don't think candidates are avoiding the issue—it just doesn't get raised." But women can raise the issue...and ask for clear answers.

• "To find out if candidates are serious about stopping rape and helping survivors, find out how much money they are willing to designate for it," says Lynn Thompson-Haas of the National Coalition Against Sexual Assault.

• The best way to gauge candidates' true positions on sexual assault may be to find out how they feel about "date" or "acquaintance" rape. "Some candidates may still believe the myths and stereotypes like, 'If a woman is out late, she's asking for it,' " says Thompson-Haas.

### FOR MORE INFORMATION

• **National Coalition Against Sexual Assault,** Box 21378, Washington, D.C. 20009. (202) 483-7165. *Monitors and advocates legislation on the national level, provides training for workers in the anti-sexual assault movement.*

• **National Network for Victims of Sexual Assault,** P.O. Box 409, Ivy, VA 22945. (804) 979-9002. *Monitors and analyzes legislation and case law developments (court rulings) at the national and state levels, facilitates a sexual assault issues network. Call or write for free brochure.*

First woman mayor in the U.S.: Susanna Salter of Argonia, Kansas, in 1887.

# RIGHT TO CHOOSE

*An estimated 70% of Americans believe abortion is a
private issue between a woman and her doctor.*

Abortion is one of the most complex issues Americans have
to face. There are people on both sides of the debate who
have sincerely held beliefs.

But whatever your personal views on abortion, the idea of *not
having a choice* is unacceptable to most women. The majority of
American women believe they have the right to decide what happens to their own bodies.

As this book was going to press, the Supreme Court was hearing
a case which could overturn *Roe v. Wade*, the landmark decision
legalizing abortion. If *Roe* is overturned, abortion laws will be
determined by state legislatures.

This is an election year; we can protect our rights by electing
pro-choice candidates in each state.

## DID YOU KNOW
• During the 1930s, an estimated 10,000 women died *every year*
from illegal abortions in the United States.

• Worldwide, illegal abortion is the leading cause of maternal
mortality (200,000 women die each year), ectopic pregnancies and
hysterectomies.

• Pro-choice voters have power. According to the National Abortion Rights Action League, in 1990 pro-choice voters were responsible for electing 4 governors, 2 senators and 8 representatives who
were pro-choice, and for restoring pro-choice majorities in the legislatures in Arizona and Idaho.

## PROGRESS REPORT
### The Supreme Court
Since the mid-1980s, the appointment of conservative justices has
led to a series of decisions chipping away at *Roe v. Wade* without
explicitly overturning it. The most recent rulings:

**1989: _Webster v. Reproductive Health Services._** Upheld the right
of states to place some restrictions on access to abortions.

In the U.S., abortion rights weren't restricted until the end of the 19th century.

**1990: _Hodgson v. Minnesota, Ohio v. Akron Center for Repro-
ductive Health._** Upheld laws requiring minors (under 18) to notify
one or both parents before they can have an abortion. The only exception: A judicial bypass, in which a young woman may go before
a judge who decides if she is "mature enough" to have an abortion).

**1991: _Rust v. Sullivan._** The so-called "gag rule" case, which
effectively prohibited workers at government-funded clinics from
discussing abortion with patients.

**1992: _Planned Parenthood of Southeastern Pennsylvania v.
Casey._** Asks the Supreme Court to rule on the constitutionality of
_Roe v. Wade._ A decision is due before the presidential election.

**State Anti-Abortion Laws**

• In 1991, bills making abortion a criminal offense were introduced
in 14 states and passed in 2—Louisiana and Utah. (However, the
two state laws are not being enforced because _Roe v. Wade_ is still in
effect.) Abortion rights are currently at risk in 25 states in which
the governor and both legislative houses want to outlaw abortion.

• At press time, a total of 33 states had passed some form of law
requiring minors (under 18) to tell or get permission from their parents before having an abortion. The laws are currently being challenged or not enforced in many states.

• Supporters of parental consent laws portray them as efforts to
foster family communication and protect young women, but that's
not what's happening. For example: In Rhode Island, which has a
parental consent law, nearly 50% of minors seeking abortions go out
of state instead of consulting their parents. And in a two-state study
(one with a parental consent law, one without), the same number of
minors told their parents.

• Parental consent laws also interfere with having abortions done
during the first trimester (the safest time). In Minnesota, delays
caused by parental consent laws resulted in a 26.5% rise in riskier
second-trimester abortions among teens.

**State Pro-Choice Laws**

• Some states (e.g., California) have anti-abortion laws on the
books that were nullified when _Roe v. Wade_ passed. Activists are
working to remove those laws in case _Roe v. Wade_ is overturned and
the states revert to the old laws.

Two days after the pro-choice march in Washington, D.C. in April, 1992, (an estimated 750,000

- In some states, lawmakers have gone further, introducing bills that protect women's right to choose. Connecticut, Washington and Maryland have passed pro-choice laws, and in Nevada, a referendum prohibited the legislature from repealing pro-choice laws.

- Other states are introducing bills that link abortion with additional reproductive rights. A Minnesota bill combines abortion rights with increased funding for family planning, better sex education in schools, and prenatal care for low-income women. Similar bills have been introduced in Ohio, Wisconsin and Pennsylvania.

### Federal Legislation

- In January 1991, 22 senators and 91 representatives introduced The Freedom of Choice Act. This bill would prohibit states from passing laws restricting women's right to have an abortion before fetal viability (about 24 weeks). If passed, it would protect women's right to choose even if the Supreme Court overturns *Roe v. Wade*.

- After the decision on *Rust v. Sullivan*, Congress passed a bill preventing the implementation of the gag rule. President Bush vetoed it, and Congress wasn't able to override the veto. Under pressure from medical groups, the Department of Health and Human Services said doctors, but not nurses, could discuss abortion if necessary.

- Reproductive rights groups and members of Congress have been trying to address the misinformation about this "compromise" on the gag rule. According to one expert, "the rule still stands and prevents everyone—physicians, nurses, etc.—from providing abortion counseling." Legislation that would repeal the gag rule is currently pending in Congress.

### Clinics

- Since the mid-1980s, abortion clinics across the country have been picketed and women have been harassed by anti-choice groups. Violence has escalated recently: In 1991, there were 8 arson attacks, and property damage was estimated at over $1 million.

- Since 1989, 15 states have introduced or passed laws prohibiting the blocking or hindering of anyone entering or leaving a medical facility. In addition, there is a bill in Congress called the Freedom of Access to Clinic Entrances bill, which would make clinic harassment a federal crime.

### RU-486

- RU-486 is an abortion-inducing drug developed in France.

people), the Bush administration recommended that the Supreme Court overturn *Roe v. Wade*.

Proponents believe its availability would make abortion as a surgical procedure almost obsolete. In addition, the drug may help fight diseases like glaucoma, breast and prostate cancer, and infertility.

• About 60% of Americans believe RU-486 should be available here, but anti-choice groups have threatened boycotts and other consequences if it's imported and tested.

## THE WOMEN'S VOTE: 1992

### 1. Political Goals

• **The right of all women to choose a safe abortion—with no restrictions.** Government should not have control over our bodies.

• **A repeal of the gag rule on federally funded family planning clinics.** This is a medical issue, not just freedom of speech issue; the gag rule prevents health care professionals from letting women know about all their options.

• **Freedom from harassment at clinics.** Women should be able to walk into a women's health clinic without feeling threatened.

• **Testing of RU-486.** If it's safe, it should be made available here.

### 2. What to Look For

• Abortion rights is of the hottest political issues of 1992. According to Barbara Radford of the National Abortion Federation, when candidates talk about their positions on abortion, listen closely to see if they qualify their views. "They may be trying to play it safe without taking a stand," she says.

• To find out where Senate incumbents stand on the gag rule, see how they voted on the Title X Pregnancy Counseling bill in the congressional scorecard section (p. 52).

## FOR MORE INFORMATION

• **National Abortion Rights Action League,** 1101 14th St. NW, 5th Floor, Washington, D.C. 20005. (202) 408-4600. *Works at the national and state levels to keep abortion safe and legal.*

• **Planned Parenthood Action Fund,** 810 7th Ave., New York, NY 10019. (212) 541-7800. *Promotes grass-roots lobbying and political activity to expand and preserve reproductive rights.*

• **Voters for Choice,** 2000 P St. NW, Suite 515, Washington, D.C. 20036. (202) 822-6640. *The largest independent pro-choice political action committee.*

# SEXUAL HARASSMENT

*About two-thirds of women polled in a recent survey said they'd been sexually harassed at work by their immediate supervisor or someone higher up.*

D id you watch the Clarence Thomas confirmation hearings on TV? For many women, they hit a raw nerve. We were appalled at the way Anita Hill was treated by the Senate Judiciary Committee...and many of us were also reminded of sexual comments and propositions we've had to deal with at work.

Many people didn't understand why women were so upset about the hearings. They asked why, if Hill had been harassed, she didn't complain at the time. But as anyone who's experienced sexual harassment may know, speaking up doesn't necessarily help. In fact, by raising the issue, a woman can damage her reputation, lose promotions, or even jeopardize her job. In one study, 90% of sexual harassment victims said they did not file a formal complaint because they were afraid of retaliation or of losing their privacy.

Women should not have to endure sexual harassment in the workplace. Politicians should be paying attention to this issue.

## DID YOU KNOW

• It's estimated that 50-85% of American women will experience some form of sexual harassment during their academic or working life.

• In a study of federal employees, 33% of women who were sexually harassed said that filing a complaint "made things worse."

• Studies show that 1/4 to 1/3 of women who make formal sexual harassment complaints are fired. In addition, an estimated 42% of harassment victims who file complaints quit their jobs because ongoing harassment made staying intolerable.

• In one study, 90% of women who were harassed reported psychological stress and 60% suffered from physical symptoms (insomnia, eating disorders, etc.).

• A 1988 survey of U.S. companies found that 90% had received complaints about sexual harassment, and more than 1/3 had been sued by the victims.

Surveys at some colleges have found that 70-80% of female students have been sexually harassed.

• However, very few sexual harassment cases are prosecuted by the government. For example, in 1990, the Equal Employment Opportunity Commission (EEOC) prosecuted only 50 of almost 6,000 complaints.

## PROGRESS REPORT

### Defining the Law

• In 1980, the EEOC defined sexual harassment as a form of sexual discrimination under Title VII of the Civil Rights Act of 1964. The number of sexual harassment complaints received by the agency skyrocketed from less than 100 to 4,280 in 1985.

• In 1986, EEOC guidelines defining sexual harassment as "conduct that creates a hostile work environment" were upheld by the Supreme Court. This allowed women to file complaints against subtle harassment (i.e., continuous sexual jokes, displaying sexually oriented posters and calendars at the office). From 1986 to 1990, complaints at the EEOC rose another 30%.

• In 1991, a federal court recognized that women react to sexual harassment differently than men, and said judges and juries have to take this into consideration. The U.S. Court of Appeals for the 9th Circuit established that the "appropriate perspective" for judging a sexual harassment case was that of a "reasonable woman."

• Also in 1991, the new Civil Rights Act allowed women who sue their employers because of sexual harassment to get some punitive damages. Before that, women could expect only back pay and coverage for out-of-pocket expenses such as medical or legal bills. This made it hard for women to find lawyers to take their cases, which can take years and are often expensive to prosecute.

• These new laws are a step in the right direction, but there are some major loopholes. For example, most state and local sexual harassment laws apply only to women working for companies with 15 or more employees...but the majority of American companies have fewer than 15 employees.

### Enforcing the Law

• Since 1985, the EEOC has prosecuted less than 1% of the sexual harassment complaints received each year. Part of the

Men and women view sexual harassment differently: In one survey, 67% of the men said they'd

problem has been the gutting of the EEOC by the government over the last decade. Since 1980, staffing has been reduced by 24%; in 1990, there were 2,853 investigators and a backlog of almost 42,000 cases.

• Currently, the typical *Fortune 500* company pays an average estimated $6.7 million per year in lost productivity, absenteeism and legal fees related to sexual harassment. But according to the National Council for Research on Women, a good sexual harassment prevention program costs much less—about $200,000. In spite of this, many companies choose to ignore the issue rather than adopt policies against harassment and enforce penalties against harassers.

• One of the biggest gaps in the enforcement picture is Congress itself. Both the Senate and the House of Representatives have exempted themselves from federal laws on sexual harassment. In 1990, the Capitol Hill Women's Political Caucus asked congressional representatives to sign a pledge promising their employees a workplace free from sexual harassment. Even after the Clarence Thomas hearings, only about 50% of the 535 members of Congress signed it.


### Settlements

• The problem with the Civil Rights Act is that it limits punitive damages for sexual harassment and other forms of sexual discrimination, depending on the size of the company being sued. This is inappropriate in light of the fact that there is no "cap" for damages awarded in other types of employment discrimination cases. Companies with 15 or fewer employees (about 80% of all companies) are exempt, and companies with 15-100 employees are only required to pay a maximum of $50,000. And the most a woman can receive—no matter how large the company or how blatant the harassment—is $300,000.

• Even in states with no caps on damages (e.g., Texas and California), settlements in sexual harassment cases are low. In Illinois settlements average only $3,234, and in California, $973.

• There is currently a bill in Congress called the Equal Remedies Act, which would remove the caps on damages in cases of sex discrimination.

be flattered by a sexual proposition from a coworker; 63% of the women said they'd be insulted.

## THE WOMEN'S VOTE: 1992

### 1. Political Goals

• **More funding for prosecuting sexual harassment cases at the EEOC.** As the nation's top enforcement agency, the EEOC should be setting a better example.

• **Passage of the Equal Remedies Act.** The caps on damages awarded for women who sue their employers for sexual harassment should be lifted.

• **Removal of the congressional exemption for sexual harassment.** Congress should not be above the law.

• **The assurance that women can safely file sexual harassment complaints.** State and federal laws should ensure that women can file complaints without being further harassed or penalized.

### 2. What to Look For

• "The Thomas hearings made most candidates aware of sexual harassment," says Ellen Bravo of 9 to 5, National Association of Working Women. "But that doesn't necessarily mean they take it seriously as a problem...or that they're in favor of strong measures to protect women."

• To find out where U.S. congressional incumbents stand, see how they voted on the 1991 Civil Rights Act (p. 52). Also check how Senators voted on the Thomas confirmation (p. 52).

• If candidates don't address sexual harassment in campaign literature or discuss it publicly, how can you tell if they're serious about preventing it? A simple test: See if they have anti-sexual harassment policies in their own offices. If they don't, find out why.

### FOR MORE INFORMATION

• **9 to 5, National Association of Working Women,** 614 Superior Ave. NW, Cleveland, OH 44113. (216) 566-9308. *A research and advocacy group for working women. Publications available on issues ranging from pregnancy discrimination to office health and safety. Also has a toll-free job problem hotline:* (800) 522-0925.

• **Fund for the Feminist Majority,** 1600 Wilson Blvd., Suite 704, Arlington, VA 22209. (703) 522-2214. *Sexual harassment hotline:* (703) 522-2501. *Call for information about publications.*

In 1991, Clarence Thomas claimed he hadn't spoken to anyone about *Roe v. Wade* for 18 years.

# CANDIDATES'

# RECORDS

# EVALUATING CANDIDATES

*It's not always easy to tell which candidates will support women's issues if they're elected. Here are tips on finding out where politicians really stand:*

## 1. Check Their Records

• According to the National Women's Political Caucus, "In some instances, candidates have committed to do more for women if elected...than their past records would indicate."

• Use this book to check U.S. congressional incumbents' voting records on key "women's bills" (p. 52-72). Check state and local candidates' records by finding out if they support the legislation listed for your state (p. 76-94). For the presidential candidates' records, see p. 50-51.

## 2. Ask Questions

Do your own candidate evaluations by asking yourself questions as you listen to speeches and debates, read newspapers and campaign literature, etc. For example:

• What bills or policies related to women's concerns has the candidate introduced, sponsored or supported?

• What activities and events does he or she attend or support that reflect a commitment to helping women?

• Are there women at all levels of her or his administration, including top decision-making posts?

• Does he or she address women's issues consistently or change positions with the publication of new opinion polls?

**Note:** You may find that the candidates aren't giving direct answers to questions like, "Do you support more funding for child care?" According to the League of Women Voters, it's not enough for them to give the issue lip service with a reply like "I've always been concerned about the availability of child care." They should

**Ten states have never elected a woman to either house of Congress.**

have a realistic plan of action and be able to discuss costs and how programs will actually work.

### 3. Beware of Buzzwords
• Listen for catchy phrases like "pro-motherhood" and "traditional values." These were coined to make candidates sound like they care about the issues you do…but they can disguise a candidate's beliefs.

• For example, "traditional values" conjures up images of happy families, job stability, adequate housing, etc.—things which aren't a reality for many people. But the term can actually refer to a very narrowly defined view of family living, with the woman at home taking care of kids. Try to translate buzzwords into what the candidates are *really* saying.

### 4. Make a Phone Call
If you still can't figure out where candidates stand on women's issues, call their campaign offices and ask for copies of their position papers on the issues most important to you.

## A NOTE ABOUT WOMEN CANDIDATES
Both men and women candidates can support women's issues; some men are very supportive and some women aren't. However, studies show that women are often more committed to passing pro-women legislation. According to a recent survey of state legislators by The Center for the American Woman in Politics:

• 74% of the male legislators said having women in the legislature had made them more aware of how issues affect women.

• 59% of the women—compared to 36% of the men—said they'd worked to pass a women's bill in the previous session.

• 60% of all legislators said having more women lawmakers had changed spending priorities.

For more information about evaluating candidates, see the election resources on pp. 95-96.

ates with the lowest percentage of women state legislators: Alabama (5.7%) and Kentucky (5.8%).

# PRESIDENTIAL CANDIDATES' RECORDS

*Here's how President Bush and the two Democratic front-runners (at press time) Bill Clinton and Jerry Brown—stand on 5 selected women's issues.*

## CHILD CARE

**George Bush:** Opposes all legislation that would require businesses to offer child care.

**Bill Clinton:** Created a child care commission in Arkansas, started the country's first child care voucher system. Helped pass the Act for Better Child Care Services in the 101st Congress. Says that if elected, he will establish a national child care network.

**Jerry Brown:** As Governor of California, made child care benefits available to all working women, augmented child care programs by $12 million a year, designated $10 million to develop new child care programs.

## FAMILY AND MEDICAL LEAVE

**George Bush:** Vetoed the 1990 Family and Medical Leave Act (see p. 52), has promised to veto the 1992 version.

**Bill Clinton:** Supports the Family and Medical Leave Act.

**Jerry Brown:** As Governor, granted California state employees a year of leave for pregnancy, childbirth and recovery.

## WOMEN'S HEALTH

**George Bush:** Has stated that he will veto the NIH Revitalization Act (see pp. 13 and 28), which would increase funding for women's health research by $90 million and require that women be included in clinical drug trials. Reason: The legislation would also lift the ban on research using fetal tissue—research that holds promise for finding cures for diseases like Parkinson's Disease, diabetes, etc.

**Bill Clinton:** According to his campaign literature, if elected, he "will increase resources available to fight breast, cervical, and other gynecological cancers."

**Jerry Brown:** Enacted legislation to maintain a prenatal health

**Sixty-four percent of new jobs created in the U.S. since 1979 have been filled by women.**

program in the Department of Health Services.

## RIGHT TO CHOOSE

**George Bush:** Recently asked the Supreme Court to overrule *Roe v. Wade*. Vetoed legislation which would have prevented implementation of the "gag rule" (see p. 40). Claims to support abortion in cases of rape, incest or threat to the mother's life, but in 1989, he vetoed a bill that would have provided Medicaid coverage for abortions in cases of rape or incest.

**Bill Clinton:** Calls himself pro-choice, says he would sign into law the Freedom of Choice Act (see p. 41) if elected. Would support federal funding for abortions in cases of rape, incest and threat to the mother's health. However, in 1989, he signed a state parental consent law.

**Jerry Brown:** Supports *Roe v. Wade*, the Freedom of Choice Act, the overturning of the gag rule, Medicaid funding for abortions.

## SEXUAL HARASSMENT

**George Bush:** Before signing the Civil Rights Act (see p. 44), he insisted that damages women can win in sex discrimination cases be limited. His administration has cut funding for the Equal Employment Opportunity Commission (EEOC) although sexual harassment cases have dramatically increased (see pp. 44-45).

**Bill Clinton:** Lobbied for a strong civil rights bill in 1991 and appointed a task force to draft complementary legislation for Arkansas.

**Jerry Brown:** Designated sexual harassment as an unfair employment practice in California.

## FOR MORE INFORMATION

• **Bush Campaign Headquarters,** 1030 15th NW, 12th Floor, Washington, D.C. 20005. (202) 336-7080.

• **Campaign Headquarters, Clinton Committee,** P.O. Box 615, Little Rock, AR 72203. (501) 372-1992.

• **Brown for President,** 2121 Cloverfield Blvd., Suite #120, Santa Monica, CA 90404-5277. (310) 449-1992.

Only 6 of the 40 U.S. presidents have appointed women to cabinet positions.

# CONGRESSIONAL SCORECARDS

*The following charts show how members of the U.S. House and Senate voted on ten (five each) representative bills affecting women. This information should be useful in helping you decide who to vote for this year. For a more complete picture, we recommend that you call your representatives' offices and find out if they support the pending legislation listed on p. 73.*

## BILLS IN THE SENATE

**1. *Family & Medical Leave Act (FMLA)/Substitute.*** (S 5, Oct. 2, 1991) In its original form, S 5 required companies with 50 or more employees to grant employees 12 weeks of job-protected unpaid leave to care for a newborn, newly-adopted child or sick relative, or to deal with their own medical problems. This substitute bill contains provisions to appease the business community. For example, it lowers potential penalties against businesses that violate the measure and allows employers to deny leave to "key employees." Although this bill is a watered-down version, a "yes" vote still gets a point. Passed 65-32, but President Bush has threatened to veto it.

**2. *Labor Health and Human Services Conference Report.*** (Nov. 7, 1991) Designates $150 million for Title X (the federal family planning program) and significant funding for women's health initiatives, with more than $10 million for the Office of Research on Women's Health. A "yes" vote gets a point. Passed 73-24, but vetoed by President Bush because it would also have postponed implementation of the "gag rule" on federally funded clinics for one year.

**3. *Title X Pregnancy Counseling.*** (July 16, 1991) An amendment codifying (making legal) the "gag rule," prohibiting federal family planning workers from providing abortion counseling and referral services. A "no" vote gets a point. Rejected 35-64.

**4. *Civil Rights.*** (Oct. 30, 1991) Makes it easier for workers to sue for employment discrimination, allows victims of sex bias to collect damages, and permits women, religious minorities and the disabled to win compensatory and punitive damages for intentional discrimination. A "yes" vote gets a point. Passed 95-5.

**5.Thomas Confirmation.** (Oct. 15, 1991) The vote to confirm Clarence Thomas to the Supreme Court. He was accused of sexual harassment by his former employee Anita Hill. A "no" vote gets a point. Confirmed 52-48.

## BILLS IN THE HOUSE OF REPRESENTATIVES

**1. Family & Medical Leave Act.** (H.R. 2, Nov. 13, 1991) Basically the same as the Senate version (see #1, Senate bills). A "yes" vote gets a point. Passed 253-177, but Bush has threatened to veto it.

**2. Labor-HHS Conference Report.** (Nov. 6, 1991) Same as Senate version (see #2 above). "Yes" gets a point. Passed 272-156, vetoed.

**3. Veto override attempt for Labor-HHS.** Bush vetoed Labor-HHS (#2 above) because it would have prevented implementation of the "gag rule" on federally funded clinics. This was an attempt to override the veto. A "yes" gets a point. Override failed, 276-156.

**4. Civil Rights.** (Nov. 7, 1991) Same as Senate version except for one provision. A "yes" gets a point. Passed, 381-38.

**5. NIH Revitalization Act.** (HR 2507, July 25, 1991) Reauthorizes programs at the National Institutes of Health (NIH) and provides funding for research on breast and ovarian cancer, osteoporosis, contraception, and infertility, and an Office of Research on Women's Health. A "yes" gets a point. Passed 274-142.

## SCORECARD KEY

Votes that support women's rights are on the left, those that don't are on the right. (On Senate bills # 3 and #5, "no" votes were actually votes *for* women's rights.) What the symbols mean:

%  = Total score on the bills (we gave 20% for each pro-women vote for a possible 100%.)

—  = No vote was cast. We tallied the remaining 4 votes. If 2 or more votes were missing, we wrote N/S ("no score").

\*  = A Senate member up for reelection. (The whole House is up.)

# ALABAMA

### U.S. Senate Bills

| | FMLA | Labor | Title X | Civ Rt | Thomas | SCORE |
|---|---|---|---|---|---|---|
| Heflin (D) | N | Y | | Y | Y | N | 60% |
| Shelby* (D) | N | Y | N | Y | | Y | 60% |

### U.S. House Bills

| | FMLA | Labor | V.O. | Civ Rt | NIH | SCORE |
|---|---|---|---|---|---|---|
| Bevill (D) | Y | Y | Y | Y | Y | 100% |
| Browder (D) | N | Y | Y | Y | Y | 80% |
| Callahan (R) | N | N | N | N | N | 0% |
| Cramer (D) | N | Y | Y | Y | Y | 80% |
| Dickinson (R) | N | Y | N | N | N | 20% |
| Erdreich (D) | Y | Y | Y | Y | Y | 100% |
| Harris (D) | N | Y | Y | Y | Y | 80% |

# ALASKA

### U.S. Senate Bills

| | FMLA | Labor | Title X | Civ Rt | Thomas | SCORE |
|---|---|---|---|---|---|---|
| Murkowski* (R) | Y | Y | | Y | Y | Y | 60% |
| Stevens (R) | Y | Y | N | Y | | Y | 80% |

### U.S. House Bills

| | FMLA | Labor | V.O. | Civ Rt | NIH | SCORE |
|---|---|---|---|---|---|---|
| Young (R) | — | | N | N | Y | N | 20% |

# ARIZONA

### U.S. Senate Bills

| | FMLA | Labor | Title X | Civ Rt | Thomas | SCORE |
|---|---|---|---|---|---|---|
| DeConcini (D) | Y | Y | | Y | Y | Y | 60% |
| McCain* (R) | Y | N | | Y | Y | Y | 40% |

### U.S. House Bills

| | FMLA | Labor | V.O. | Civ Rt | NIH | SCORE |
|---|---|---|---|---|---|---|
| Kolba (R) | N | N | Y | Y | Y | 60% |
| Kyi (R) | N | N | N | Y | N | 20% |
| Pastor (D) | Y | Y | Y | Y | N | 80% |
| Rhodes (R) | N | N | N | Y | N | 20% |
| Stump (R) | N | N | N | N | N | 0% |

# ARKANSAS

### U.S. Senate Bills

| | FMLA | Labor | Title X | Civ Rt | Thomas | SCORE |
|---|---|---|---|---|---|---|
| Bumpers* (D) | Y | Y | N | Y | N | 100% |
| Pryor (D) | — | Y | — | Y | N | N/S |

Y/N at left=Vote supporting women's rights; Y/N at right=Vote not supporting women's right
See pp. 52-53 for scorecard key and descriptions of bills.

# ARKANSAS (cont.)

## U.S. House Bills

| | FMLA | Labor | V.O. | Clv Rt | NIH | SCORE |
|---|---|---|---|---|---|---|
| Alexander (D) | Y | Y | Y | Y | Y | 100% |
| Anthony (D) | Y | Y | Y | — | Y | 80% |
| Hammerschmidt (R) | N | N | N | N | Y | 20% |
| Thorton (D) | Y | Y | Y | Y | Y | 100% |

# CALIFORNIA

## U.S. Senate Bills

| | FMLA | Labor | Title X | Clv Rt | Thomas | SCORE |
|---|---|---|---|---|---|---|
| Cranston (D) | Y | — | N | Y | N | 80% |
| Seymour* (R) | N | Y | N | Y | Y | 60% |

## U.S. House Bills

| | FMLA | Labor | V.O. | Clv Rt | NIH | SCORE |
|---|---|---|---|---|---|---|
| Anderson (D) | Y | Y | Y | Y | Y | 100% |
| Beilenson (D) | Y | Y | Y | Y | Y | 100% |
| Berman (D) | Y | Y | Y | Y | Y | 100% |
| Boxer (D) | Y | Y | Y | — | Y | 80% |
| Brown (D) | Y | Y | Y | Y | Y | 100% |
| Campbell (R) | Y | Y | Y | Y | — | 80% |
| Condit (D) | Y | Y | Y | Y | Y | 100% |
| Cox (R) | N | N | N | Y | N | 20% |
| Cunningham (R) | N | N | N | Y | N | 20% |
| Dannemeyer (R) | N | N | N | — | N | 0% |
| Dellums (D) | Y | Y | Y | Y | Y | 100% |
| Dixon (D) | Y | Y | Y | Y | Y | 100% |
| Dooley (D) | Y | Y | Y | Y | Y | 100% |
| Doolittle (R) | N | N | N | N | N | 0% |
| Dornan (R) | N | N | N | Y | N | 20% |
| Dreier (R) | N | N | N | Y | N | 20% |
| Dymally (D) | Y | Y | Y | Y | Y | 100% |
| Edwards (D) | Y | Y | Y | Y | Y | 100% |
| Fazio (D) | Y | Y | Y | Y | Y | 100% |
| Gallegley (R) | N | N | N | Y | N | 20% |
| Herger (R) | N | N | N | N | N | 0% |
| Hunter (R) | N | N | N | Y | N | 20% |
| Lagomarsino (R) | N | N | N | Y | N | 20% |
| Lantos (D) | Y | Y | Y | Y | Y | 100% |
| Lehman (D) | Y | Y | Y | Y | Y | 100% |
| Levine (D) | Y | Y | — | — | Y | N/S |
| Lewis (R) | N | N | N | Y | N | 20% |
| Lowery (R) | N | N | N | Y | N | 20% |
| Martinez (D) | Y | — | Y | Y | Y | 80% |
| Matsui (D) | Y | Y | Y | — | Y | 80% |
| McCandless (R) | N | Y | Y | Y | N | 60% |
| Miller (D) | Y | Y | Y | Y | Y | 100% |
| Mineta (D) | Y | Y | Y | Y | Y | 100% |
| Moorhead (R) | N | N | N | Y | N | 20% |
| Packard (R) | N | N | N | Y | N | 20% |
| Panetta (D) | Y | Y | Y | Y | Y | 100% |

Y/N at left=Vote supporting women's rights; Y/N at right=Vote not supporting women's rights.
See pp. 52-53 for scorecard key and descriptions of bills.

# CALIFORNIA (cont.)

| | FMLA | Labor | V.O. | Civ Rt | NIH | SCORE |
|---|---|---|---|---|---|---|
| Pelosi (D) | Y | Y | Y | Y | Y | 100% |
| Riggs (R) | N | N | Y | Y | Y | 60% |
| Rohrabacher (R) | N | N | N | N | N | 0% |
| Roybal (D) | Y | Y | Y | Y | Y | 100% |
| Stark (D) | Y | Y | Y | Y | Y | 100% |
| Thomas (R) | N | N | Y | Y | Y | 60% |
| Torres (D) | Y | Y | Y | Y | Y | 100% |
| Waters (D) | Y | Y | Y | Y | Y | 100% |
| Waxman (D) | Y | Y | Y | Y | Y | 100% |

# COLORADO
### U.S. Senate Bills

| | FMLA | Labor | Title X | Civ Rt | Thomas | SCORE |
|---|---|---|---|---|---|---|
| Brown (R) | N | Y | N | Y | Y | 60% |
| Wirth* (D) | Y | Y | N | Y | N | 100% |

### U.S. House Bills

| | FMLA | Labor | V.O. | Civ Rt | NIH | SCORE |
|---|---|---|---|---|---|---|
| Allard (R) | N | N | N | N | N | 0% |
| Campbell (D) | Y | Y | Y | Y | Y | 100% |
| Hefley (R) | N | N | N | N | N | 0% |
| Schaefer (R) | N | N | N | Y | N | 20% |
| Schroeder (D) | Y | Y | Y | Y | Y | 100% |
| Skaggs (D) | Y | Y | Y | Y | Y | 100% |

# CONNECTICUT
### U.S. Senate Bills

| | FMLA | Labor | Title X | Civ Rt | Thomas | SCORE |
|---|---|---|---|---|---|---|
| Dodd* (D) | Y | Y | N | Y | N | 100% |
| Lieberman (D) | Y | Y | N | Y | N | 100% |

### U.S. House Bills

| | FMLA | Labor | V.O. | Civ Rt | NIH | SCORE |
|---|---|---|---|---|---|---|
| DeLaura (D) | Y | Y | Y | Y | Y | 100% |
| Franks (R) | N | Y | Y | Y | — | 60% |
| Gelderson (D) | Y | — | Y | Y | Y | 80% |
| Johnson (R) | Y | Y | Y | Y | Y | 100% |
| Kennelly (D) | Y | Y | Y | Y | Y | 100% |
| Shays (R) | Y | Y | Y | Y | Y | 100% |

# DELAWARE
### U.S. Senate Bills

| | FMLA | Labor | Title X | Civ Rt | Thomas | SCORE |
|---|---|---|---|---|---|---|
| Biden (D) | Y | Y | N | Y | N | 100% |
| Roth (R) | Y | N | N | Y | Y | 60% |

Y/N at left=Vote supporting women's rights; Y/N at right=Vote not supporting women's rights.
See pp. 52-53 for scorecard key and descriptions of bills.

# DELAWARE (cont.)

## U.S. House Bills

| | FMLA | Labor | V.O. | Civ Rt | NIH | SCORE |
|---|---|---|---|---|---|---|
| Carper (D) | Y | Y | Y | Y | Y | 100% |

# FLORIDA

## U.S. Senate Bills

| | FMLA | Labor | Title X | Civ Rt | Thomas | SCORE |
|---|---|---|---|---|---|---|
| Graham* (D) | Y | Y | N | Y | N | 100% |
| Mack (R) | N | N | Y | Y | Y | 20% |

## U.S. House Bills

| | FMLA | Labor | V.O. | Civ Rt | NIH | SCORE |
|---|---|---|---|---|---|---|
| Bacchus (D) | Y | Y | Y | Y | Y | 100% |
| Bennett (D) | Y | N | N | Y | Y | 60% |
| Bilirakis (R) | N | N | N | Y | N | 20% |
| Fascell (D) | Y | Y | Y | Y | Y | 100% |
| Gibbons (D) | Y | Y | Y | Y | Y | 100% |
| Goss (R) | N | N | N | Y | N | 20% |
| Hutto (D) | N | N | N | Y | N | 20% |
| Ireland (R) | N | N | N | Y | N | 20% |
| James (R) | Y | N | N | Y | N | 40% |
| Johnston (D) | Y | Y | Y | Y | Y | 100% |
| Lehman (D) | Y | Y | Y | Y | Y | 100% |
| Lewis (R) | N | N | N | Y | N | 20% |
| McCollum (R) | N | N | N | Y | N | 20% |
| Peterson (D) | Y | Y | Y | Y | Y | 100% |
| Ros-Lehtinen (R) | Y | N | N | Y | N | 40% |
| Shaw (R) | N | N | N | Y | N | 20% |
| Smith (D) | Y | Y | Y | — | Y | 80% |
| Stearns (R) | N | N | N | N | N | 0% |
| Young (R) | N | N | N | Y | N | 20% |

# GEORGIA

## U.S. Senate Bills

| | FMLA | Labor | Title X | Civ Rt | Thomas | SCORE |
|---|---|---|---|---|---|---|
| Fowler* (D) | Y | Y | N | Y | Y | 80% |
| Nunn (D) | Y | Y | N | Y | Y | 80% |

## U.S. House Bills

| | FMLA | Labor | V.O. | Civ Rt | NIH | SCORE |
|---|---|---|---|---|---|---|
| Barnard (D) | N | N | N | Y | Y | 40% |
| Darden (D) | N | Y | Y | Y | Y | 80% |
| Gingrich (R) | N | N | N | Y | N | 20% |
| Hatcher (D) | — | Y | — | Y | Y | N/S |
| Jenkins (D) | Y | Y | Y | Y | Y | 100% |
| Jones (D) | N | Y | Y | Y | Y | 80% |

Y/N at left=Vote supporting women's rights; Y/N at right=Vote not supporting women's rights.
See pp. 52-53 for scorecard key and descriptions of bills.

# GEORGIA (cont.)
### U.S. House Bills (cont.)

| | FMLA | Labor | V.O. | Civ Rt | NIH | SCORE |
|---|---|---|---|---|---|---|
| Lewis (D) | Y | Y | Y | Y | Y | 100% |
| Ray (D) | N | N | N | Y | N | 20% |
| Rowland (D) | N | Y | Y | Y | Y | 80% |
| Thomas (D) | N | Y | Y | Y | Y | 80% |

# HAWAII
### U.S. Senate Bills

| | FMLA | Labor | Title X | Civ Rt | Thomas | SCORE |
|---|---|---|---|---|---|---|
| Akaka (D) | Y | Y | N | Y | N | 100% |
| Inouye* (D) | Y | Y | N | Y | N | 100% |

### U.S. House Bills

| | FMLA | Labor | V.O. | Civ Rt | NIH | SCORE |
|---|---|---|---|---|---|---|
| Abercrombie (D) | Y | Y | Y | N | Y | 80% |
| Mink (D) | Y | Y | Y | N | Y | 80% |

# IDAHO
### U.S. Senate Bills

| | FMLA | Labor | Title X | Civ Rt | Thomas | SCORE |
|---|---|---|---|---|---|---|
| Craig (R) | N | N | Y | Y | Y | 20% |
| Symms (R) | N | N | Y | N | Y | 0% |

### U.S. House Bills

| | FMLA | Labor | V.O. | Civ Rt | NIH | SCORE |
|---|---|---|---|---|---|---|
| LaRocco (D) | N | Y | — | Y | Y | 60% |
| Stallings (D) | N | N | N | Y | Y | 40% |

# ILLINOIS
### U.S. Senate Bills

| | FMLA | Labor | Title X | Civ Rt | Thomas | SCORE |
|---|---|---|---|---|---|---|
| Dixon (D) | Y | Y | N | Y | Y | 80% |
| Simon (D) | Y | Y | N | Y | N | 100% |

### U.S. House Bills

| | FMLA | Labor | V.O. | Civ Rt | NIH | SCORE |
|---|---|---|---|---|---|---|
| Annunzio (D) | Y | N | N | Y | Y | 60% |
| Bruce (D) | Y | Y | Y | Y | Y | 100% |
| Collins (D) | Y | Y | Y | Y | Y | 100% |
| Costello (D) | Y | N | N | Y | Y | 60% |
| Cox (D) | Y | Y | Y | Y | Y | 100% |
| Crane (R) | N | N | N | N | N | 0% |
| Durbin (D) | Y | Y | Y | Y | Y | 100% |
| Evans (D) | Y | Y | Y | Y | Y | 100% |
| Ewing (R) | N | N | N | Y | N | 20% |
| Fawell (R) | N | Y | Y | Y | N | 60% |

**Y/N at left=Vote supporting women's rights; Y/N at right=Vote not supporting women's rights.**
See pp. 52-53 for scorecard key and descriptions of bills.

# ILLINOIS (cont.)

## U.S. House Bills (cont.)

| | FMLA | Labor | V.O. | Civ Rt | NIH | SCORE |
|---|---|---|---|---|---|---|
| Hastert (R) | N | N | N | Y | N | 20% |
| Hayes (D) | Y | Y | Y | Y | Y | 100% |
| Hyde (R) | Y | N | N | Y | N | 40% |
| Lipinski (D) | Y | N | N | N | Y | 40% |
| Michel (R) | N | N | N | Y | N | 20% |
| Porter (R) | N | Y | Y | Y | Y | 80% |
| Poshard (D) | Y | N | N | Y | Y | 60% |
| Rostenkowski (D) | Y | Y | Y | Y | Y | 100% |
| Russo (D) | Y | Y | Y | N | Y | 80% |
| Sangmeister (D) | Y | — | Y | — | Y | N/S |
| Savage (D) | Y | Y | Y | Y | Y | 100% |
| Yates (D) | Y | Y | Y | Y | Y | 100% |

# INDIANA

## U.S. Senate Bills

| | FMLA | Labor | Title X | Civ Rt | Thomas | SCORE |
|---|---|---|---|---|---|---|
| Coats* (R) | Y | N | Y | N | Y | 20% |
| Lugar (R) | N | N | Y | Y | Y | 20% |

## U.S. House Bills

| | FMLA | Labor | V.O. | Civ Rt | NIH | SCORE |
|---|---|---|---|---|---|---|
| Burton (R) | N | N | N | Y | N | 20% |
| Hamilton (D) | N | Y | Y | Y | Y | 80% |
| Jacobs (D) | Y | Y | Y | Y | Y | 100% |
| Jontz (D) | Y | Y | Y | Y | Y | 100% |
| Long (D) | Y | Y | Y | Y | Y | 100% |
| McCloskey (D) | Y | Y | Y | Y | Y | 100% |
| Myers (R) | N | Y | Y | Y | N | 60% |
| Roemer (D) | Y | Y | Y | Y | N | 80% |
| Sharp (D) | Y | Y | Y | Y | Y | 100% |
| Visclosky (D) | Y | Y | Y | Y | Y | 100% |

# IOWA

## U.S. Senate Bills

| | FMLA | Labor | Title X | Civ Rt | Thomas | SCORE |
|---|---|---|---|---|---|---|
| Harkin (D) | — | Y | N | Y | N | 80% |
| Grassley* (R) | N | Y | Y | Y | Y | 40% |

## U.S. House Bills

| | FMLA | Labor | V.O. | Civ Rt | NIH | SCORE |
|---|---|---|---|---|---|---|
| Grandy (R) | N | Y | Y | Y | N | 60% |
| Leach (R) | Y | Y | Y | Y | Y | 100% |
| Lightfoot (R) | N | N | N | Y | N | 20% |
| Nagle (D) | Y | Y | Y | Y | Y | 100% |
| Nussle (R) | N | N | N | Y | N | 20% |
| Smith (D) | Y | Y | Y | Y | Y | 100% |

Y/N at left=Vote supporting women's rights; Y/N at right=Vote not supporting women's rights.
See pp. 52-53 for scorecard key and descriptions of bills.

# KANSAS

### U.S. Senate Bills

| | FMLA | Labor | Title X | Civ Rt | Thomas | SCORE |
|---|---|---|---|---|---|---|
| Dole* (R) | N | N | Y | Y | Y | 20% |
| Kassebaum (R) | N | Y | N | Y | Y | 60% |

### U.S. House Bills

| | FMLA | Labor | V.O. | Civ Rt | NIH | SCORE |
|---|---|---|---|---|---|---|
| Glickman (D) | N | Y | Y | Y | Y | 80% |
| Meyers (R) | N | Y | Y | Y | Y | 80% |
| Nichols (R) | N | N | N | N | N | 0% |
| Roberts (R) | N | N | N | N | N | 0% |
| Slattery (D) | N | Y | Y | Y | Y | 80% |

# KENTUCKY

### U.S. Senate Bills

| | FMLA | Labor | Title X | Civ Rt | Thomas | SCORE |
|---|---|---|---|---|---|---|
| Ford* (D) | Y | N | Y | Y | N | 60% |
| McConnell (R) | N | Y | Y | Y | Y | 40% |

### U.S. House Bills

| | FMLA | Labor | V.O. | Civ Rt | NIH | SCORE |
|---|---|---|---|---|---|---|
| Bunning (R) | N | N | N | — | N | 0% |
| Hopkins (R) | N | — | N | — | — | N/S |
| Hubbard (D) | Y | Y | Y | Y | Y | 100% |
| Mazzoli (D) | Y | N | N | Y | Y | 60% |
| Natcher (D) | Y | Y | Y | Y | Y | 100% |
| Perkins (D) | Y | Y | Y | Y | Y | 100% |
| Rogers (R) | N | N | N | Y | N | 20% |

# LOUISIANA

### U.S. Senate Bills

| | FMLA | Labor | Title X | Civ Rt | Thomas | SCORE |
|---|---|---|---|---|---|---|
| Breaux* (D) | Y | N | Y | Y | Y | 40% |
| Johnston (D) | Y | N | Y | Y | Y | 40% |

### U.S. House Bills

| | FMLA | Labor | V.O. | Civ Rt | NIH | SCORE |
|---|---|---|---|---|---|---|
| Baker (R) | N | N | N | N | N | 0% |
| Hayes (D) | N | — | N | — | N | N/S |
| Holloway (R) | N | N | N | N | — | 0% |
| Huckaby (D) | N | N | N | Y | Y | 40% |
| Jefferson (D) | Y | Y | Y | Y | Y | 100% |
| Livingston (R) | N | N | N | N | N | 0% |
| McCrery (R) | N | N | N | Y | — | 20% |
| Tauzin (D) | N | N | N | Y | N | 20% |

Y/N at left=Vote supporting women's rights; Y/N at right=Vote not supporting women's rights.
See pp. 52-53 for scorecard key and descriptions of bills.

# MAINE

### U.S. Senate Bills

| | FMLA | Labor | Title X | Civ Rt | Thomas | SCORE |
|---|---|---|---|---|---|---|
| Cohen (R) | Y | Y | N | Y | Y | 80% |
| Mitchell (D) | Y | Y | N | Y | N | 100% |

### U.S. House Bills

| | FMLA | Labor | V.O. | Civ Rt | NIH | SCORE |
|---|---|---|---|---|---|---|
| Andrews (D) | Y | Y | Y | Y | Y | 100% |
| Snowe (R) | Y | Y | Y | Y | Y | 100% |

# MARYLAND

### U.S. Senate Bills

| | FMLA | Labor | Title X | Civ Rt | Thomas | SCORE |
|---|---|---|---|---|---|---|
| Mikulski* (D) | Y | Y | N | Y | N | 100% |
| Sarbanes (D) | Y | Y | N | Y | N | 100% |

### U.S. House Bills

| | FMLA | Labor | V.O. | Civ Rt | NIH | SCORE |
|---|---|---|---|---|---|---|
| Bentley (R) | N | Y | Y | Y | Y | 80% |
| Byron (D) | N | Y | Y | Y | Y | 80% |
| Cardin (D) | Y | Y | Y | Y | Y | 100% |
| Gilchrest (R) | N | Y | Y | Y | Y | 80% |
| Hoyer (D) | Y | Y | Y | Y | Y | 100% |
| McMillen (D) | Y | Y | Y | Y | Y | 100% |
| Mfume (D) | Y | Y | Y | Y | Y | 100% |
| Morello (R) | Y | Y | Y | Y | Y | 100% |

# MASSACHUSETTS

### U.S. Senate Bills

| | FMLA | Labor | Title X | Civ Rt | Thomas | SCORE |
|---|---|---|---|---|---|---|
| Kennedy (D) | Y | Y | N | Y | N | 100% |
| Kerry (D) | Y | Y | N | Y | N | 100% |

### U.S. House Bills

| | FMLA | Labor | V.O. | Civ Rt | NIH | SCORE |
|---|---|---|---|---|---|---|
| Atkins (D) | Y | Y | Y | Y | Y | 100% |
| Donnelly (D) | Y | N | N | Y | Y | 60% |
| Early (D) | Y | Y | Y | Y | Y | 100% |
| Frank (D) | Y | Y | Y | Y | Y | 100% |
| Kennedy (D) | Y | Y | Y | Y | Y | 100% |
| Markey (D) | Y | Y | Y | Y | Y | 100% |
| Mavroules (D) | Y | N | N | Y | Y | 60% |
| Moakley (D) | Y | Y | Y | Y | Y | 100% |
| Neal (D) | Y | Y | Y | Y | Y | 100% |
| Olver (D) | Y | Y | Y | Y | Y | 100% |
| Studds (D) | Y | Y | Y | Y | Y | 100% |

Y/N at left=Vote supporting women's rights; Y/N at right=Vote not supporting women's rights.
See pp. 52-53 for scorecard key and descriptions of bills.

# MICHIGAN

## U.S. Senate Bills

| | FMLA | Labor | Title X | Civ Rt | Thomas | SCORE |
|---|---|---|---|---|---|---|
| Levin (D) | Y | Y | N | Y | N | 100% |
| Riegle (D) | Y | Y | N | Y | N | 100% |

## U.S. House Bills

| | FMLA | Labor | V.O. | Civ Rt | NIH | SCORE |
|---|---|---|---|---|---|---|
| Bonior (D) | Y | Y | Y | Y | Y | 100% |
| Broomfield (R) | N | N | N | Y | N | 20% |
| Camp (R) | N | N | N | Y | N | 20% |
| Carr (D) | N | Y | Y | Y | Y | 80% |
| Collins (D) | Y | Y | Y | Y | Y | 100% |
| Conyers (D) | Y | Y | Y | Y | Y | 100% |
| Davis (R) | Y | N | N | Y | N | 40% |
| Dingell (D) | Y | Y | Y | Y | Y | 100% |
| Ford (D) | Y | Y | Y | Y | Y | 100% |
| Henry (R) | N | N | N | Y | N | 20% |
| Hertel (D) | Y | Y | Y | Y | Y | 100% |
| Kildee (D) | Y | Y | N | Y | Y | 80% |
| Levin (D) | Y | Y | Y | Y | Y | 100% |
| Pursell (R) | N | Y | Y | Y | Y | 80% |
| Traxler (D) | Y | Y | Y | Y | Y | 100% |
| Upton (R) | N | Y | Y | Y | Y | 80% |
| Vander Jagt (R) | N | N | N | N | N | 0% |
| Wolpe (D) | Y | Y | Y | Y | Y | 100% |

# MINNESOTA

## U.S. Senate Bills

| | FMLA | Labor | Title X | Civ Rt | Thomas | SCORE |
|---|---|---|---|---|---|---|
| Durenberger (R) | Y | N | Y | Y | Y | 40% |
| Wellstone (D) | Y | Y | N | Y | N | 100% |

## U.S. House Bills

| | FMLA | Labor | V.O. | Civ Rt | NIH | SCORE |
|---|---|---|---|---|---|---|
| Oberstar (D) | Y | Y | N | — | Y | 60% |
| Penny (D) | N | Y | Y | Y | N | 60% |
| Peterson (D) | Y | N | Y | Y | Y | 80% |
| Ramstad (R) | Y | Y | Y | Y | N | 80% |
| Sabo (D) | Y | Y | Y | Y | Y | 100% |
| Sikorski (D) | Y | Y | Y | Y | Y | 100% |
| Vento (D) | Y | Y | Y | Y | Y | 100% |
| Weber (R) | N | N | N | Y | N | 20% |

# MISSISSIPPI

## U.S. Senate Bills

| | FMLA | Labor | Title X | Civ Rt | Thomas | SCORE |
|---|---|---|---|---|---|---|
| Cochran (R) | N | Y | Y | Y | Y | 40% |
| Lott (R) | N | N | Y | Y | Y | 20% |

Y/N at left=Vote supporting women's rights; Y/N at right=Vote not supporting women's rights
See pp. 52-53 for scorecard key and descriptions of bills.

# MISSISSIPPI (cont.)

## U.S. House Bills

| | FMLA | Labor | V.O. | Civ Rt | NIH | SCORE |
|---|---|---|---|---|---|---|
| Espy (D) | Y | Y | Y | Y | Y | 100% |
| Montgomery (D) | N | N | N | Y | N | 20% |
| Parker (D) | N | N | N | Y | N | 20% |
| Taylor (D) | N | N | N | Y | N | 20% |
| Whitten (D) | N | Y | Y | Y | Y | 80% |

# MISSOURI

## U.S. Senate Bills

| | FMLA | Labor | Title X | Civ Rt | Thomas | SCORE |
|---|---|---|---|---|---|---|
| Bond* (R) | Y | Y | N | Y | Y | 80% |
| Danforth (R) | Y | Y | Y | Y | Y | 60% |

## U.S. House Bills

| | FMLA | Labor | V.O. | Civ Rt | NIH | SCORE |
|---|---|---|---|---|---|---|
| Clay (D) | Y | Y | Y | Y | Y | 100% |
| Coleman (R) | N | Y | Y | Y | N | 60% |
| Emerson (R) | N | N | N | Y | N | 20% |
| Gephardt (D) | Y | Y | Y | Y | Y | 100% |
| Hancock (R) | N | N | N | N | N | 0% |
| Horn (D) | Y | Y | Y | Y | Y | 100% |
| Skelton (D) | N | Y | Y | Y | N | 60% |
| Volkmer (D) | Y | N | N | Y | N | 40% |
| Wheat (D) | Y | Y | Y | Y | Y | 100% |

# MONTANA

## U.S. Senate Bills

| | FMLA | Labor | Title X | Civ Rt | Thomas | SCORE |
|---|---|---|---|---|---|---|
| Baucus (D) | Y | Y | N | Y | N | 100% |
| Burns (R) | N | N | Y | Y | Y | 20% |

## U.S. House Bills

| | FMLA | Labor | V.O. | Civ Rt | NIH | SCORE |
|---|---|---|---|---|---|---|
| Marlenee (R) | N | N | N | N | N | 0% |
| Williams (D) | Y | Y | Y | Y | Y | 100% |

# NEBRASKA

## U.S. Senate Bills

| | FMLA | Labor | Title X | Civ Rt | Thomas | SCORE |
|---|---|---|---|---|---|---|
| Exon (D) | Y | Y | Y | Y | Y | 60% |
| Kerrey (D) | — | — | N | — | N | N/S |

## U.S. House Bills

| | FMLA | Labor | V.O. | Civ Rt | NIH | SCORE |
|---|---|---|---|---|---|---|
| Barrett (R) | N | N | N | Y | N | 20% |
| Bereuter (R) | N | Y | Y | Y | N | 60% |
| Hoagland (D) | Y | Y | Y | Y | Y | 100% |

Y/N at left=Vote supporting women's rights; Y/N at right=Vote not supporting women's rights.
See pp. 52-53 for scorecard key and descriptions of bills.

# NEVADA
## U.S. Senate Bills

| | FMLA | Labor | Title X | Civ Rt | Thomas | SCORE |
|---|---|---|---|---|---|---|
| Bryan (D) | Y | Y | N | Y | N | 100% |
| Reid* (D) | Y | Y | Y | Y | N | 80% |

## U.S. House Bills

| | FMLA | Labor | V.O. | Civ Rt | NIH | SCORE |
|---|---|---|---|---|---|---|
| Bilbray (D) | Y | Y | Y | Y | Y | 100% |
| Vucanovich (R) | N | N | N | Y | N | 20% |

# NEW HAMPSHIRE
## U.S. Senate Bills

| | FMLA | Labor | Title X | Civ Rt | Thomas | SCORE |
|---|---|---|---|---|---|---|
| Rudman* (R) | N | Y | N | Y | Y | 60% |
| Smith (R) | N | N | Y | N | Y | 0% |

## U.S. House Bills

| | FMLA | Labor | V.O. | Civ Rt | NIH | SCORE |
|---|---|---|---|---|---|---|
| Swett (D) | Y | Y | Y | Y | Y | 100% |
| Zeliff (R) | N | Y | Y | N | N | 40% |

# NEW JERSEY
## U.S. Senate Bills

| | FMLA | Labor | Title X | Civ Rt | Thomas | SCORE |
|---|---|---|---|---|---|---|
| Bradley (D) | Y | Y | N | Y | N | 100% |
| Launtenberg (D) | Y | Y | N | Y | N | 100% |

## U.S. House Bills

| | FMLA | Labor | V.O. | Civ Rt | NIH | SCORE |
|---|---|---|---|---|---|---|
| Andrews (D) | Y | Y | Y | Y | Y | 100% |
| Dwyer (D) | Y | Y | Y | Y | Y | 100% |
| Gallo (R) | N | Y | Y | Y | Y | 80% |
| Guarini (D) | Y | Y | Y | Y | Y | 100% |
| Hughes (D) | Y | Y | Y | Y | Y | 100% |
| Pallone (D) | Y | Y | Y | Y | Y | 100% |
| Payne (D) | Y | Y | Y | Y | Y | 100% |
| Rinaldo (R) | Y | N | N | Y | N | 40% |
| Roe (D) | Y | N | N | Y | N | 40% |
| Roukema (R) | Y | Y | Y | Y | Y | 100% |
| Saxton (R) | N | N | N | Y | N | 20% |
| Smith (R) | Y | N | N | Y | N | 40% |
| Torricelli (D) | Y | Y | Y | Y | Y | 100% |
| Zimmer (R) | Y | Y | Y | Y | Y | 100% |

Y/N at left=Vote supporting women's rights; Y/N at right=Vote not supporting women's rights.
See pp. 52-53 for scorecard key and descriptions of bills.

# NEW MEXICO

## U.S. Senate Bills

| | FMLA | Labor | Title X | Civ Rt | Thomas | SCORE |
|---|---|---|---|---|---|---|
| Bingaman (D) | Y | Y | N | Y | N | 100% |
| Domenici (R) | N | N | Y | Y | Y | 20% |

## U.S. House Bills

| | FMLA | Labor | V.O. | Civ Rt | NIH | SCORE |
|---|---|---|---|---|---|---|
| Richardson (D) | Y | Y | Y | Y | Y | 100% |
| Schiff (R) | N | Y | Y | Y | Y | 80% |
| Skeen (R) | N | Y | Y | Y | Y | 80% |

# NEW YORK

## U.S. Senate Bills

| | FMLA | Labor | Title X | Civ Rt | Thomas | SCORE |
|---|---|---|---|---|---|---|
| D'Amato (R) | Y | Y | Y | Y | Y | 60% |
| Moynihan (D) | Y | Y | N | Y | N | 100% |

## U.S. House Bills

| | FMLA | Labor | V.O. | Civ Rt | NIH | SCORE |
|---|---|---|---|---|---|---|
| Ackerman (D) | Y | Y | Y | Y | Y | 100% |
| Boehlert (R) | Y | Y | Y | Y | Y | 100% |
| Downey (D) | Y | Y | Y | Y | Y | 100% |
| Engel (D) | Y | Y | Y | Y | Y | 100% |
| Fish (R) | Y | Y | Y | Y | N | 80% |
| Flake (D) | Y | Y | Y | Y | Y | 100% |
| Gilman (R) | Y | Y | Y | Y | Y | 100% |
| Green (R) | Y | Y | Y | Y | Y | 100% |
| Hochbrueckner (D) | Y | Y | Y | Y | Y | 100% |
| Horton (R) | Y | Y | Y | Y | Y | 100% |
| Houghton (R) | N | Y | Y | Y | Y | 80% |
| LaFalce (D) | Y | N | N | Y | Y | 60% |
| Lent (R) | N | N | N | Y | N | 20% |
| Lowey (D) | Y | Y | Y | Y | Y | 100% |
| Manton (D) | Y | N | N | Y | Y | 60% |
| Martin (R) | Y | Y | Y | Y | Y | 100% |
| McGrath (R) | Y | N | N | Y | N | 40% |
| McHugh (D) | Y | Y | Y | Y | Y | 100% |
| McNulty (D) | Y | Y | Y | Y | Y | 100% |
| Molinari (R) | Y | Y | Y | Y | Y | 100% |
| Mrazek (D) | Y | Y | Y | Y | — | 80% |
| Nowak (D) | Y | N | N | Y | Y | 60% |
| Owens (D) | Y | Y | Y | Y | Y | 100% |
| Paxon (R) | N | N | N | Y | N | 20% |
| Rangel (D) | Y | Y | Y | Y | Y | 100% |
| Scheur (D) | Y | Y | Y | Y | Y | 100% |
| Schumer (D) | Y | Y | Y | Y | Y | 100% |
| Serrano (D) | Y | Y | Y | Y | Y | 100% |

Y/N at left=Vote supporting women's rights; Y/N at right=Vote not supporting women's rights.
See pp. 52-53 for scorecard key and descriptions of bills.

# NEW YORK (cont.)

### U.S. House Bills (cont.)

| | FMLA | Labor | V.O. | Civ Rt | NIH | SCORE |
|---|---|---|---|---|---|---|
| Slaughter (D) | Y | Y | Y | Y | Y | 100% |
| Solarz (D) | Y | Y | Y | Y | Y | 100% |
| Solomon (R) | Y | N | N | Y | N | 40% |
| Towns (D) | Y | Y | Y | Y | Y | 100% |
| Walsh (R) | N | N | N | Y | N | 20% |
| Weiss (D) | Y | Y | Y | — | — | N/S |

# NORTH CAROLINA

### U.S. Senate Bills

| | FMLA | Labor | Title X | Civ Rt | Thomas | SCORE |
|---|---|---|---|---|---|---|
| Helms (R) | N | N | Y | N | Y | 0% |
| Sanford* (D) | Y | Y | N | Y | N | 100% |

### U.S. House Bills

| | FMLA | Labor | V.O. | Civ Rt | NIH | SCORE |
|---|---|---|---|---|---|---|
| Ballenger (R) | N | N | N | Y | N | 20% |
| Coble (R) | N | N | N | Y | N | 20% |
| Hefner (D) | Y | Y | Y | Y | — | 80% |
| Jones (D) | Y | Y | Y | Y | Y | 100% |
| Lancaster (D) | N | Y | Y | Y | N | 60% |
| McMillan (R) | N | N | N | Y | N | 20% |
| Neal (D) | N | Y | Y | Y | N | 60% |
| Price (D) | Y | Y | Y | Y | Y | 100% |
| Rose (D) | Y | Y | Y | Y | Y | 100% |
| Taylor (R) | N | N | N | Y | N | 20% |
| Valentine (D) | N | Y | Y | Y | Y | 80% |

# NORTH DAKOTA

### U.S. Senate Bills

| | FMLA | Labor | Title X | Civ Rt | Thomas | SCORE |
|---|---|---|---|---|---|---|
| Burdick (D) | Y | Y | N | Y | N | 100% |
| Conrad* (D) | Y | Y | N | Y | N | 100% |

### U.S. House Bills

| | FMLA | Labor | V.O. | Civ Rt | NIH | SCORE |
|---|---|---|---|---|---|---|
| Dorgan (D) | Y | Y | Y | Y | Y | 100% |

# OHIO

### U.S. Senate Bills

| | FMLA | Labor | Title X | Civ Rt | Thomas | SCORE |
|---|---|---|---|---|---|---|
| Glenn* (D) | Y | Y | N | Y | N | 100% |
| Metzenbaum (D) | Y | Y | N | Y | N | 100% |

### U.S. House Bills

| | FMLA | Labor | V.O. | Civ Rt | NIH | SCORE |
|---|---|---|---|---|---|---|
| Applegate (D) | Y | N | N | Y | N | 40% |
| Boehner (R) | N | N | N | N | N | 0% |

Y/N at left=Vote supporting women's rights; Y/N at right=Vote not supporting women's rig
See pp. 52-53 for scorecard key and descriptions of bills.

## U.S. House Bills (cont.)

| | FMLA | Labor | V.O. | Civ Rt | NIH | SCORE |
|---|---|---|---|---|---|---|
| Eckart (D) | Y | Y | Y | Y | Y | 100% |
| Feighan (D) | Y | Y | Y | Y | Y | 100% |
| Gillmor (R) | Y | N | N | Y | N | 40% |
| Gradison (R) | N | N | Y | — | N | 20% |
| Hall (D) | Y | N | N | Y | N | 40% |
| Hobson (R) | N | Y | Y | Y | Y | 80% |
| Kaptur (D) | Y | Y | Y | Y | Y | 100% |
| Kasich (R) | N | N | N | Y | N | 20% |
| Luken (D) | N | N | N | Y | N | 20% |
| McEwen (R) | N | N | N | N | N | 0% |
| Miller (R) | N | N | N | Y | N | 20% |
| Oakar (D) | Y | Y | Y | Y | Y | 100% |
| Oxley (R) | N | N | N | N | N | 0% |
| Pease (D) | Y | Y | Y | Y | Y | 100% |
| Regula (R) | Y | Y | Y | Y | N | 80% |
| Sawyer (D) | Y | Y | Y | Y | Y | 100% |
| Stokes (D) | Y | Y | Y | Y | Y | 100% |
| Traficant (D) | Y | Y | Y | Y | Y | 100% |
| Wylie (R) | N | N | N | N | N | 0% |

# OKLAHOMA

## U.S. Senate Bills

| | FMLA | Labor | Title X | Civ Rt | Thomas | SCORE |
|---|---|---|---|---|---|---|
| Boren (D) | N | Y | Y | Y | Y | 40% |
| Nickles* (R) | N | N | Y | Y | Y | 20% |

## U.S. House Bills

| | FMLA | Labor | V.O. | Civ Rt | NIH | SCORE |
|---|---|---|---|---|---|---|
| Brewster (D) | N | Y | Y | Y | Y | 80% |
| Edwards (R) | N | N | N | Y | N | 20% |
| English (D) | Y | Y | Y | Y | Y | 100% |
| Inhofe (R) | N | N | N | N | N | 0% |
| McCurdy (D) | Y | Y | Y | Y | Y | 100% |
| Synar (D) | Y | Y | Y | Y | Y | 100% |

# OREGON

## U.S. Senate Bills

| | FMLA | Labor | Title X | Civ Rt | Thomas | SCORE |
|---|---|---|---|---|---|---|
| Hatfield (R) | Y | Y | N | Y | Y | 80% |
| Packwood* (R) | Y | Y | N | Y | N | 100% |

## U.S. House Bills

| | FMLA | Labor | V.O. | Civ Rt | NIH | SCORE |
|---|---|---|---|---|---|---|
| AuCoin (D) | Y | Y | Y | Y | Y | 100% |
| DeFazio (D) | Y | Y | Y | Y | Y | 100% |
| Kopetski (D) | Y | Y | Y | Y | Y | 100% |
| Smith (R) | N | N | N | Y | N | 20% |
| Wyden (D) | Y | Y | Y | Y | Y | 100% |

**Y/N at left=Vote supporting women's rights; Y/N at right=Vote not supporting women's rights. See pp. 52-53 for scorecard key and descriptions of bills.**

# PENNSYLVANIA

## U.S. Senate Bills

| | FMLA | Labor | Title X | Civ Rt | Thomas | SCORE |
|---|---|---|---|---|---|---|
| Specter* (R) | Y | Y | N | Y | Y | 80% |
| Wofford (D) | Y | Y | N | — | N | 80% |

## U.S. House Bills

| | FMLA | Labor | V.O. | Civ Rt | NIH | SCORE |
|---|---|---|---|---|---|---|
| Blackwell (D) | Y | — | Y | Y | — | N/S |
| Borski (D) | Y | N | N | Y | Y | 60% |
| Clinger (R) | N | Y | Y | Y | N | 60% |
| Coughlin (R) | Y | Y | Y | Y | N | 80% |
| Coyne (D) | Y | Y | Y | Y | Y | 100% |
| Foglietta (D) | Y | Y | Y | Y | Y | 100% |
| Gaydos (D) | Y | N | Y | Y | — | 60% |
| Gekas (R) | N | Y | Y | Y | Y | 80% |
| Goodling (R) | N | Y | Y | Y | N | 60% |
| Kanjorski (D) | Y | N | N | Y | N | 40% |
| Kolter (D) | Y | N | N | Y | N | 40% |
| Kostmayer (D) | Y | Y | Y | Y | Y | 100% |
| McDade (R) | Y | N | N | Y | N | 40% |
| Murphy (D) | Y | N | N | Y | N | 40% |
| Murtha (D) | Y | Y | Y | Y | N | 80% |
| Ridge (R) | N | Y | Y | Y | Y | 80% |
| Ritter (R) | N | N | N | Y | N | 20% |
| Santorum (R) | N | N | N | Y | N | 20% |
| Schulze (R) | — | N | N | Y | Y | 40% |
| Shuster (R) | N | N | N | N | N | 0% |
| Walker (R) | N | N | N | Y | N | 20% |
| Weldon (R) | Y | Y | N | Y | N | 60% |
| Yatron (D) | Y | N | N | Y | — | 40% |

# RHODE ISLAND

## U.S. Senate Bills

| | FMLA | Labor | Title X | Civ Rt | Thomas | SCORE |
|---|---|---|---|---|---|---|
| Chafee (R) | Y | Y | N | Y | Y | 80% |
| Pell (D) | Y | Y | N | Y | N | 100% |

## U.S. House Bills

| | FMLA | Labor | V.O. | Civ Rt | NIH | SCORE |
|---|---|---|---|---|---|---|
| Machtley (R) | Y | Y | Y | Y | — | 80% |
| Reed (D) | Y | Y | Y | Y | Y | 100% |

# SOUTH CAROLINA

## U.S. Senate Bills

| | FMLA | Labor | Title X | Civ Rt | Thomas | SCORE |
|---|---|---|---|---|---|---|
| Hollings* (D) | N | Y | N | Y | Y | 60% |
| Thurmond (R) | N | N | Y | Y | Y | 20% |

Y/N at left=Vote supporting women's rights; Y/N at right=Vote not supporting women's rights
See pp. 52-53 for scorecard key and descriptions of bills.

# SOUTH CAROLINA (cont.)

## U.S. House Bills

| | FMLA | Labor | V.O. | Civ Rt | NIH | SCORE |
|---|---|---|---|---|---|---|
| Derrick (D) | N | Y | Y | Y | Y | 80% |
| Patterson (D) | N | Y | Y | Y | Y | 80% |
| Ravenel (R) | Y | Y | Y | Y | Y | 100% |
| Spence (R) | N | N | N | Y | Y | 40% |
| Spratt (D) | Y | Y | Y | Y | Y | 100% |
| Tallon (D) | Y | N | N | Y | N | 40% |

# SOUTH DAKOTA

## U.S. Senate Bills

| | FMLA | Labor | Title X | Civ Rt | Thomas | SCORE |
|---|---|---|---|---|---|---|
| Daschle* (D) | Y | Y | N | Y | N | 100% |
| Pressler (R) | N | N | Y | Y | Y | 20% |

## U.S. House Bills

| | FMLA | Labor | V.O. | Civ Rt | NIH | SCORE |
|---|---|---|---|---|---|---|
| Johnson (D) | Y | Y | Y | Y | Y | 100% |

# TENNESSEE

## U.S. Senate Bills

| | FMLA | Labor | Title X | Civ Rt | Thomas | SCORE |
|---|---|---|---|---|---|---|
| Gore (D) | Y | Y | N | Y | N | 100% |
| Sasser (D) | Y | Y | N | Y | N | 100% |

## U.S. House Bills

| | FMLA | Labor | V.O. | Civ Rt | NIH | SCORE |
|---|---|---|---|---|---|---|
| Clement (D) | Y | Y | Y | Y | Y | 100% |
| Cooper (D) | N | Y | Y | Y | Y | 80% |
| Duncan (R) | N | N | N | Y | N | 20% |
| Ford (D) | Y | Y | Y | Y | Y | 100% |
| Gordon (D) | Y | Y | Y | Y | Y | 100% |
| Lloyd (D) | N | Y | Y | Y | Y | 80% |
| Quillen (R) | N | N | N | Y | — | 20% |
| Sundquist (R) | N | N | N | Y | — | 20% |
| Tanner (D) | N | Y | Y | Y | Y | 80% |

# TEXAS

## U.S. Senate Bills

| | FMLA | Labor | Title X | Civ Rt | Thomas | SCORE |
|---|---|---|---|---|---|---|
| Bentsen (D) | Y | Y | N | Y | N | 100% |
| Gramm (R) | N | N | Y | Y | Y | 20% |

**Y/N at left=Vote supporting women's rights; Y/N at right=Vote not supporting women's rights.**
See pp. 52-53 for scorecard key and descriptions of bills.

# TEXAS (cont.)

## U.S. House Bills

| | FMLA | Labor | V.O. | Civ Rt | NIH | SCORE |
|---|---|---|---|---|---|---|
| Andrews (D) | Y | Y | Y | Y | Y | 100% |
| Archer (R) | N | N | N | N | N | 0% |
| Armey (R) | N | N | N | N | N | 0% |
| Barton (R) | N | N | N | Y | N | 20% |
| Brooks (D) | Y | Y | Y | Y | Y | 100% |
| Bryant (D) | Y | Y | Y | Y | Y | 100% |
| Bustamante (D) | Y | Y | Y | Y | Y | 100% |
| Chapman (D) | Y | Y | Y | Y | Y | 100% |
| Coleman (D) | Y | Y | Y | Y | Y | 100% |
| Combest (R) | N | N | N | N | N | 0% |
| de la Garza (D) | Y | N | N | Y | Y | 60% |
| DeLay (R) | N | N | N | N | N | 0% |
| Edwards (D) | N | Y | Y | Y | Y | 80% |
| Fields (R) | N | N | N | N | N | 0% |
| Frost (D) | Y | Y | Y | Y | Y | 100% |
| Geren (D) | N | Y | Y | Y | Y | 80% |
| Gonzalez (D) | Y | Y | Y | N | Y | 80% |
| Hall (D) | N | N | N | Y | Y | 40% |
| Johnson (R) | N | N | N | Y | Y | 40% |
| Laughlin (D) | N | Y | Y | Y | Y | 80% |
| Ortiz (D) | Y | N | N | Y | Y | 60% |
| Pickle (D) | Y | Y | Y | Y | Y | 100% |
| Sarpalius (D) | N | N | N | Y | Y | 40% |
| Smith (R) | Y | Y | Y | Y | Y | 100% |
| Stenholm (D) | N | N | N | Y | Y | 40% |
| Washington (D) | Y | Y | Y | Y | Y | 100% |
| Wilson (D) | Y | Y | Y | Y | — | 80% |

# UTAH

## U.S. Senate Bills

| | FMLA | Labor | Title X | Civ Rt | Thomas | SCORE |
|---|---|---|---|---|---|---|
| Garn* (R) | N | N | Y | Y | Y | 20% |
| Hatch (R) | N | — | Y | Y | Y | 20% |

## U.S. House Bills

| | FMLA | Labor | V.O. | Civ Rt | NIH | SCORE |
|---|---|---|---|---|---|---|
| Hansen (R) | N | N | N | Y | N | 20% |
| Orton (D) | N | N | N | Y | — | 20% |
| Owens (D) | Y | Y | Y | Y | Y | 100% |

# VERMONT

## U.S. Senate Bills

| | FMLA | Labor | Title X | Civ Rt | Thomas | SCORE |
|---|---|---|---|---|---|---|
| Jeffords (R) | Y | Y | N | Y | N | 100% |
| Leahy* (D) | Y | Y | N | Y | N | 100% |

Y/N at left=Vote supporting women's rights; Y/N at right=Vote not supporting women's rights
See pp. 52-53 for scorecard key and descriptions of bills.

# VERMONT (cont.)

## U.S. House Bills

| | FMLA | Labor | V.O. | Civ Rt | NIH | SCORE |
|---|---|---|---|---|---|---|
| Sanders (Ind.) | Y | Y | Y | Y | Y | 100% |

# VIRGINIA

## U.S. Senate Bills

| | FMLA | Labor | Title X | Civ Rt | Thomas | SCORE |
|---|---|---|---|---|---|---|
| Robb (D) | Y | Y | N | Y | Y | 80% |
| Warner (R) | N | Y | N | Y | Y | 60% |

### U.S. House Bills

| | FMLA | Labor | V.O. | Civ Rt | NIH | SCORE |
|---|---|---|---|---|---|---|
| Allen (R) | N | Y | — | — | — | N/S |
| Bateman (R) | N | N | N | N | N | 0% |
| Bliley (R) | N | N | N | N | N | 0% |
| Boucher (D) | Y | Y | Y | Y | Y | 100% |
| Moran (D) | Y | Y | Y | Y | Y | 100% |
| Olin (D) | N | Y | Y | — | Y | 60% |
| Payne (D) | N | Y | Y | Y | Y | 80% |
| Pickett (D) | N | Y | Y | Y | Y | 80% |
| Sisisky (D) | N | Y | Y | Y | Y | 80% |
| Wolf (R) | N | N | N | Y | N | 20% |

# WASHINGTON

## U.S. Senate Bills

| | FMLA | Labor | Title X | Civ Rt | Thomas | SCORE |
|---|---|---|---|---|---|---|
| Adams (D) | Y | Y | N | Y | N | 100% |
| Gorton (R) | N | Y | N | Y | Y | 60% |

### U.S. House Bills

| | FMLA | Labor | V.O. | Civ Rt | NIH | SCORE |
|---|---|---|---|---|---|---|
| Chandler (R) | N | Y | Y | Y | Y | 80% |
| Dicks (D) | — | Y | Y | Y | Y | 80% |
| Foley (D) | — | — | Y | — | — | N/S |
| McDermott (D) | Y | Y | Y | Y | Y | 100% |
| Miller (R) | Y | Y | Y | Y | Y | 100% |
| Morrison (R) | Y | Y | Y | Y | Y | 100% |
| Swift (D) | Y | Y | Y | Y | Y | 100% |
| Unsoeld (D) | Y | Y | Y | Y | Y | 100% |

Y/N at left=Vote supporting women's rights; Y/N at right=Vote not supporting women's rights.
See pp. 52-53 for scorecard key and descriptions of bills.

# WEST VIRGINIA

### U.S. Senate Bills

| | FMLA | Labor | Title X | Civ Rt | Thomas | SCORE |
|---|---|---|---|---|---|---|
| Byrd (D) | Y | Y | N | Y | N | 100% |
| Rockefeller (D) | Y | Y | N | Y | N | 100% |

### U.S. House Bills

| | FMLA | Labor | V.O. | Civ Rt | NIH | SCORE |
|---|---|---|---|---|---|---|
| Mollohan (D) | Y | N | N | Y | N | 40% |
| Rahall (D) | Y | Y | Y | Y | N | 80% |
| Staggers (D) | Y | N | N | Y | N | 40% |
| Wise (D) | Y | Y | Y | Y | Y | 100% |

# WISCONSIN

### U.S. Senate Bills

| | FMLA | Labor | Title X | Civ Rt | Thomas | SCORE |
|---|---|---|---|---|---|---|
| Kasten* (R) | N | N | Y | Y | Y | 20% |
| Kohl (D) | Y | Y | N | Y | N | 100% |

### U.S. House Bills

| | FMLA | Labor | V.O. | Civ Rt | NIH | SCORE |
|---|---|---|---|---|---|---|
| Aspin (D) | N | Y | Y | Y | Y | 80% |
| Gunderson (R) | N | Y | Y | Y | N | 60% |
| Kleczka (D) | Y | Y | Y | Y | Y | 100% |
| Klug (R) | Y | Y | Y | Y | Y | 100% |
| Moody (D) | Y | Y | Y | Y | — | 80% |
| Obey (D) | Y | Y | Y | Y | Y | 100% |
| Petri (R) | N | N | N | Y | N | 20% |
| Roth (R) | N | N | N | Y | N | 20% |
| Sensenbrenner (R) | N | N | N | N | N | 0% |

# WYOMING

### U.S. Senate Bills

| | FMLA | Labor | Title X | Civ Rt | Thomas | SCORE |
|---|---|---|---|---|---|---|
| Simpson (R) | N | Y | N | Y | Y | 60% |
| Wallop (R) | N | N | Y | N | Y | 0% |

### U.S. House Bills

| | FMLA | Labor | V.O. | Civ Rt | NIH | SCORE |
|---|---|---|---|---|---|---|
| Thomas (R) | N | N | N | Y | N | 20% |

**Y/N at left=Vote supporting women's rights; Y/N at right=Vote not supporting women's rights.**
**See pp. 52-53 for scorecard key and descriptions of bills.**

# LEGISLATION PENDING IN CONGRESS

*The congressional scorecards represent only a small percentage of the bills concerning women in the 102nd Congress. For a more comprehensive picture of where incumbents stand on women's issues, call their offices and ask if they support these bills currently in Congress. Note: You can reach any representative's office through the congressional switchboard: (202) 224-3121.*

HR/S 25: **Freedom of Choice Act.** *Would protect the reproductive rights of women even if Roe v.Wade is overturned.*

HR 875/S 2268: **RU 486 Regulatory Fairness Act.** *Would make the FDA (Food and Drug Administration) import alert on RU486 ineffective.*

HR 1161/S 514: **Women's Health Equity Act.** *22 bills regarding women's health in the areas of research, services and prevention.*

HR 1502/S 15: **Violence Against Women Act.** *A comprehensive bill that would extend civil rights protection to victims of gender-motivated crimes and authorize funds to educate judges and prosecutors on domestic violence.*

HR 1703/S 798: **Freedom of Access to Clinic Entrances.** *Would make it a federal crime to block the entrance of a medical clinic.*

HR 3090/S 323: **Title X Reauthorization Act/Title X Pregnancy Counseling Act.** *Would overturn the "gag rule" on federal family planning clinics. Has passed in the Senate but not the House.*

HR 3526: **Economic Equity Act.** *Includes 24 provisions addressing women's economic needs.*

HR 3975/S 2053: **Equal Remedies Act.** *Would remove the cap on damages available to victims of sex discrimination.*

HJ Res 1/SJ Res 3: **Equal Rights Amendment (ERA).** *Would make women and men equal under the Constitution.*

Three states have women governors: Kansas, Oregon and Texas.

# ABOUT LOCAL CANDIDATES

• According to the American Association of University Women, "local elections, which can be decided by a margin of 50 votes or fewer, often have the greatest impact on women's lives. These elections determine property taxes, social services, and the quality of education."

• This means it's especially important to pay attention to who's running for office in your area, and to use your vote to elect pro-women candidates.

• To help you do this, we've included a "local candidate report card" (see opposite page). This page can be photocopied to make forms for each candidate you want to evaluate.

• Use the report card to rate the candidate on each issue listed. If you can't get enough details from newspapers, campaign literature, etc., call the candidate's campaign office.

## GET THE WORD OUT

Since it often takes only a few votes to determine a local election, you may want to share what you've learned about the candidates with other women in your area. Copy your report cards and distribute them to friends and co-workers. A local women's organization may even be interested in helping you make the information more widely available.

The 2 women now in the Senate: Nancy Landon Kassebaum (R-KS) and Barbara Mikulski (D-M)

# LOCAL CANDIDATE REPORT CARD: WOMEN'S ISSUES

**Candidate's Name** _____

**Running For:** _____

**Campaign Manager** _____ **Phone** _____

Scoring Key: 1=Not supportive, 2=Barely supportive, 3=Neutral, 4=Fairly supportive, 5=Very supportive

| | | | | | |
|---|---|---|---|---|---|
| Breast Cancer | 1 | 2 | 3 | 4 | 5 |
| Child Care | 1 | 2 | 3 | 4 | 5 |
| Child Support | 1 | 2 | 3 | 4 | 5 |
| Domestic Violence | 1 | 2 | 3 | 4 | 5 |
| Family Leave | 1 | 2 | 3 | 4 | 5 |
| Health Insurance | 1 | 2 | 3 | 4 | 5 |
| Medical Research | 1 | 2 | 3 | 4 | 5 |
| Pay Equity | 1 | 2 | 3 | 4 | 5 |
| Rape | 1 | 2 | 3 | 4 | 5 |
| Right to Choose | 1 | 2 | 3 | 4 | 5 |
| Sexual Harassment | 1 | 2 | 3 | 4 | 5 |

• What has the candidate done in the community to support women's issues? _____

_____

• Does the candidate publicly address women's concerns in speeches or campaign literature? _____

_____

• Is the candidate favored or endorsed by local women's organizations? Which ones? _____

_____

_____

**Women age 65 and older in the work force are paid 65% of what men in the same group earn.**

# STATE

# LEGISLATIVE
# SUMMARIES

# STATE LEGISLATIVE SUMMARIES

*We called women's groups in all 50 states and asked them to list, by order of priority, what they considered to be the most important women's issues currently being debated in their legislatures. Here's the information they provided (current at press time).*

## ALABAMA

**1. Low-Income Women.** A family of 3 in Alabama currently receives a monthly AFDC (Aid to Families with Dependent Children) payment of $149—the second lowest level in the country. A provision will be introduced in the General Fund Budget that would allocate a 16% increase for AFDC each year for the next 3 years. Passage possible.

**2. Right to Choose.** Senate Bill 267/House Bill 477 would ban abortion—with the exception of reported rape, incest, or if the pregnancy is a threat to the mother's life. Passage possible.

**FOR MORE INFORMATION:** Alabama Arise, P.O. Box 612, Montgomery, AL 36101. (205) 832-9060. *Has information on women and poverty. Free newsletter.*
• Mary Weidler, Action Chair for the League of Women Voters of Alabama, 1722 Hill Hedge Dr., Montgomery, AL 36106. *Newsletter available during the legislative session (begins February 1993). Cost: $25.*

## ALASKA

**1. Right to Choose.** HJR 58 would allow the "abortion pill," RU 486, to be sold in Alaska. Passage possible.

**2. Domestic Violence.** House Bill 156 would ensure confidentiality for victims of domestic violence and their counselors. In House Judiciary Committee. Passage possible.

**3. Family Leave.** House Bill 78 would provide 18 weeks of unpaid leave for government and school district employees. Not likely to pass.

**FOR MORE INFORMATION:** Alaska Women's Lobby, P.O. Box 22156, Juneau, AK 99802. *Newsletter available for $1. Phone: (907) 463-6744 (during legislative session January-May). June-December: Call the Alaska Network on Domestic Violence and Sexual Assault at (907) 586-3650.*

Women are 11% and men are 7% more likely to vote for a woman than a man candidate.

# ARIZONA

**1. Family Planning.** Senate Bill 1414 originally would have designated $500,000 in family planning funds for low-income women. The amount of funding has since dropped to $250,000. Has passed in the Senate, likely to pass in the House.

**2. Prenatal Care.** House Bill 2502 would channel donations given to the state into a fund for prenatal care for low-income women. Passage likely.

**FOR MORE INFORMATION:** Planned Parenthood of Central and Northern Arizona, 5651 N. 7th St., Phoenix, AZ 85014. (602) 277-7526. *Free newsletter.*

# ARKANSAS

**1. Low-Income Women.** Arkansas has the 6th-lowest welfare payment schedule in the U.S. Politicians aren't making the issue a priority, so women's organizations are pushing for reforms.

**2. Right to Choose.** A petition drive will continue through July to get an amendment prohibiting state intervention in reproductive choice on the ballot. For details, call the ACLU at (501) 374-2660.

**FOR MORE INFORMATION:** Arkansas Women's Political Caucus, P.O. Box 2494, Little Rock, AR 72203. 324-9495. *Write for free newsletter.*

# CALIFORNIA

**1. Low-Income Women.** Governor Wilson's proposed Taxpayer Protection Initiative would drastically cut welfare, making it difficult for families to meet basic housing and food needs. If it doesn't pass the legislature (it's not likely to pass), it will go on the popular ballot in November.

**2. Right to Choose.** In 1987, Assembly Bill 2274 was passed requiring minors to get parental consent or a judicial bypass before an abortion. The ACLU and National Center for Youth Law are challenging its constitutionality. A decision is expected some time this summer, but the case will probably be appealed and be decided in the state Supreme Court.

**FOR MORE INFORMATION:** CARAL North, 300 Brannan St. #501, San Francisco, CA 94107. (415) 546-7211. CARAL South, 225 Santa Monica Blvd. #406, Santa Monica, CA 90401. (310) 393-0513. *Both have free newsletters.*

• National Organization for Women—State Chapter, 926 J St., Suite 523, Sacramento, CA 95814. (916) 442-3414.

State with the highest percentage of women legislators: Arizona (34%).

# COLORADO

**1. Health Care.** Senate Bill 4 would fund a study on the feasibility of insurance for all residents. Passed in both houses, governor likely to sign.

**2. Support for Low-Income Women.** Senate Bill 62, introduced by Senator Gallagher, would have increased payments for Aid to Families with Dependent Children (AFDC) by 4% and required the upgrading of payment schedules in accordance with a cost-of-living study. Status: Died.

**FOR MORE INFORMATION:** Denver Women's Commission, 303 W. Colfax, Suite 1600, Denver, CO 80204. (303) 640-3955. *Free bulletins.*

# CONNECTICUT

**1. Violence Against Women.** In the works: An initiative to increase funding for community crisis services and strengthen the civil and criminal justice system's response to domestic violence, sexual assault, and sexual harassment.

**2. Child Support.** Lobbyists are proposing the consolidation of 5 agencies involved in enforcing child support to make it easier to track down parents who don't pay. Status: Being drafted.

**3. Family Planning.** The governor recently earmarked $500,000 for family planning services to make up for federal funding that organizations like Planned Parenthood will have to give up when they violate the "gag rule."

**FOR MORE INFORMATION:** Commission on the Status of Women, 90 Washington St., Hartford, CT 06106. (203) 566-5702. *Free fact sheets.*

# DELAWARE

**1. Family Leave.** The Family Care Act (Senate Bill 122) would provide employees with up to 90 days of unpaid leave over a period of 2 years without risk of termination. Passed the Senate twice, now in the House.

**2. Gender Balance.** SCR 83 was a resolution requiring equal numbers of women and men on state boards and commissions. It was tabled; new legislation will focus on key committees and contain stronger wording.

**FOR MORE INFORMATION:** Agenda for Delaware Women, P.O. Box 1580, Wilmington, DE 19899. (302) 479-1672. *Free newsletter for members.*

**The number of women heading key state agencies fell from 149 in 1989 to 113 in 1991.**

# FLORIDA

**1. Gender Balance.** Senate Bill 940 would require that if a state board has more men than women, the next appointment must be a woman until the board is balanced. Passage possible.

**2. Sexual Harassment.** Senate Bill 1345 would legally define sexual harassment and require offices and businesses with 15+ employees to post sexual harassment policies, provide a toll-free information number. Passed House.

**3. Stalking.** House Bill 97 and Senate Bill 196 would criminalize the act of following and harassing someone. Status: Passage likely.

**FOR MORE INFORMATION:** Florida Association of Planned Parenthood, 1704 Thomasville Rd. #209, Tallahassee, FL 32303-5708. (904) 668-8009. *Free newsletter.*

# GEORGIA

**1. Right to Choose.** House Bill 767, introduced by Rep. Titus, would have required a doctor to administer anaesthesia to the fetus during abortion to "alleviate organic pain." Did not pass.

• House Bill 1062 would have required that women wait 24 hours and hear a state-mandated lecture before abortions. No vote, did not pass.

**2. Wills and Pregnant Women.** Previously, anyone with a living will who slipped into a coma, vegetative state or advanced stages of disease could request to be disconnected from life-sustaining equipment—but pregnant women were exempt. House Bill 968 overturned the exemption up to the fifth month of pregnancy; it was passed and signed by the governor.

**FOR MORE INFORMATION:** Georgians For Choice, P.O. Box 8551, Atlanta, GA 30306. (404) 607-7959.

# HAWAII

**1. Domestic Violence.** Domestic violence has reached epidemic proportions in Hawaii, so the House and Senate Women's Caucus has introduced a package of bills that, among other things, would require convicted first-time batterers to get counseling. Status: Not likely to pass.

• Funds for domestic violence programs have been drastically cut and need to be restored. No legislation drafted yet.

**FOR MORE INFORMATION:** Hawaii State Commission on the Status of Women, 335 Merchant St. #253, Honolulu, HI 96813. (808) 586-5757. *Free newsletter.*

**Women hold 28 of 435 seats in the House of Representatives.**

# IDAHO

**1. Women's Health.** Senate Bill 1392 would have required that health insurance policies covering maternity benefits also cover these benefits for dependent daughters. Defeated.

**2. Gender Balance.** Senate Bill 1401 would have required that "if at all possible," appointive commissions and boards be balanced by gender. Never debated.

**FOR MORE INFORMATION:** Idaho Women's Network, P.O. Box 1385, Boise, ID 83701. (208) 344-5738. *Free newsletter for members.*

# ILLINOIS

**1. Family Leave.** House Bill 50 and Senate Bill 25 would require employers with 50+ workers to allow up to 8 weeks of unpaid leave. Status: Has passed legislature 3 times; Governor Edgar has vetoed it each time.

**2. Low-Income Women.** Senator Watson is proposing legislation to limit women on welfare to compensation for one child. It's not likely to pass.

**FOR MORE INFORMATION:** Illinois Planned Parenthood Council, 123 S. 7th St. #400, Springfield, IL 62701. (217) 522-6776. *Write for a free legislative update.*

# INDIANA

*Note: Indiana Legislature adjourned February 14. Some of the bills passed:*

**1. Women's Health.** Senate Bill 391 will require the state employee insurance plan to cover diagnostic services, outpatient treatment and rehabilitation for women with breast cancer.

**2. Breast Cancer Detection.** Senate Bill 129 will require high school students to learn about breast (and testicular) cancer and receive instruction on self-exams.

**FOR MORE INFORMATION:** Indianapolis NOW, P.O. Box 20601, Indianapolis, IN 46220-0601. (317) 925-4641.

The number of women holding two or more jobs increased fivefold between 1970 and 1989.

# IOWA

**1. Sexual Harassment.** Senate File 316 will criminalize sexual harassment of state employees, people in the care or custody of state employees or institutions, and people attending state educational facilities. Signed by governor, takes effect July 1, 1992.

**2. Family Leave.** House File 2026 would make maternity and family leave available to public and private employees. Status: Tabled.

**3. Right to Choose.** Senate File 2253 would have mandated parental notification for minors seeking abortions. Status: Dead for this session.

**FOR MORE INFORMATION:** Iowa Planned Parenthood Affiliate League, P.O. Box 4557, Des Moines, IA 50306. (515) 280-7004. *Free quarterly newsletter.*

# KANSAS

**1. Sexual Exploitation.** House Bill 24256 would amend laws on sexual battery and aggravated sexual battery, make sexual exploitation a felony instead of a misdemeanor. Has a 50/50 chance of passing.

• House Bill 2253 would require professionals at mental health institutions to report cases of patients being exploited by other professionals. Would also remove liability on the part of the reporter. Likely to pass.

**2. Right to Choose.** House Bill 2778 would have nullified pre-*Roe v.Wade* legislation criminalizing abortion and prohibited blocking access to clinics. Status: Dead, but a similar bill is on the governor's desk.

**FOR MORE INFORMATION:** ACLU of Kansas and Western Missouri, 201 Wyandotte #209, Kansas City, MO 64105. (816) 421-4449. *Free legislative alert.*

# KENTUCKY

**1. Domestic Violence.** House Bill 115 would expand the Domestic Orders Act to include sexual abuse in the definition of domestic violence and include people who live or have lived together. Status: Will probably pass.

**2. Family Resources.** Senate Bill 86 would provide counseling and referral (except for contraceptive and family planning counseling) to school-age students and their families. Status: In House Education Committee.

**3. Right to Choose.** Senate Bill 115 would require minors to get a parent's written consent before an abortion. House Bill 479A is similar but would allow for judiciary bypass. Both in Senate Judiciary Committee.

Iowa and North Dakota now require equal numbers of women and men on state boards.

written consent before an abortion. House Bill 479A is similar but would allow for judiciary bypass. Both in Senate Judiciary Committee.

**FOR MORE INFORMATION:** Pro-choice Coalition for Kentucky, P.O. Box 995, Louisville, KY 40201. *Free newsletter.*

# LOUISIANA

**1. Child Care.** Certain child care centers (including religion-based) have more lenient licensing guidelines than others. A number of bills will be introduced to set up a single-class licensing system.

**2. Right to Choose.** State law now prohibits abortions except for victims of rape and incest. A court has ruled that the law is unconstitutional and can't be enforced. However, the state has appealed the decision and the issue is likely to come up again once the fate of *Roe v. Wade* is determined.

**FOR MORE INFORMATION:** Leslie Gerwin, 1540 Harmony St., New Orleans, LA 70115. (504) 897-9417.

# MAINE

**1. Support for Low-Income Women.** Governor McKernan's proposed budget includes drastic cuts in programs (e.g. Medicaid, job training, child care) for low-income women and children.

**2. Women and Employment.** The Non-Traditional Occupations Act (LD 2381) would designate 25% of state and federal job training funds to recruit, train, and place women in "nontraditionally female fields" like construction. Status: Referred to Senate Committee.

**3. Right to Choose.** There's talk of introducing legislation to protect women's right to abortion; nothing drafted yet.

**FOR MORE INFORMATION:** Maine Women's Lobby, P.O. Box 15, Hallowell, ME 04347. (207) 622-0851. *Free newsletter and legislative alerts.*

# MARYLAND

**1. Family Leave.** House Bill 1190 would provide unpaid family leave to certain employees who've worked at least 12 months for a minimum of 20 hours per week. Has been introduced 3 times, stalled.

**2. Violence Against Women.** House Bill 781 would have required custodians of police and court records to delete the names and identities of victims of violent crimes before passing the records along. Status: Has died.

• House Bill 505 and Senate Bill 332 would require that a person charged with a sexual offense be tested for HIV at the victim's request. Passed, awaiting governor's signature.

**3. Right to Choose.** Maryland has a referendum on the popular ballot to codify *Roe v. Wade* into state law, thereby keeping abortion legal in the state.

FOR MORE INFORMATION: Maryland Commission for Women, 311 W. Saratoga St., Baltimore, MD 21201. (410) 333-0054. *Free newsletter.*

# MASSACHUSETTS

**1. Sexual Harassment.** House Bill 2620 would require employers with 6+ employees to provide information/training on sexual harassment. Passage likely.

**2. Right to Choose.** House Bill 1337 would affirm women's fundamental right to make their own reproductive decisions. Passage possible.

**3. Clinic Access.** Senate Bill 179 would make it illegal to block entry to a medical facility in violation of a court order (above and beyond laws relating to violation of court orders). Status: In committee, has a 50/50 chance of passing.

FOR MORE INFORMATION: Women's Statewide Legislative Network of Massachusetts, 37 Temple Place, Boston, MA 02111. (617) 426-1878. *Newsletter for members.*

# MICHIGAN

**1. Right to Choose.** Senate Bill 141 would require doctors to give women having abortions information describing pregnancy and abortion procedures written by the American College of Gynecologists & Obstetricians. Status: In Conference Committee.

**2. Women's Health.** House Bill 4074 would establish education and grant programs for breast cancer and regulate the use of mammography machines. Passed in 1989, however the Department of Health has not made it a priority.

**3. Sex Discrimination.** Senate Bill 351 would allow women to join all-male country and golf clubs to take advantage of business networking opportunities. Status: In Conference Committee.

FOR MORE INFORMATION: Michigan Alliance for Choice, 19400 W. 10 Mile Rd. #107, Southfield, MI 48075. (313) 827-4550. *Newsletter for members.*

**The most popular business magazine in the country is *Working Woman*.**

## MINNESOTA

**1. Right to Choose.** House File 342 would have urged the U.S. Congress to enact the Freedom of Choice Act, which would essentially guarantee women the rights protected under *Roe v. Wade*. Did not pass.

**2. Health Care.** House File 2 will provide health care coverage for Minnesota's uninsured and underinsured. Passed.

**3. Child Support.** Senate Bill 1727 would have required the revoking of driving, hunting and fishing licenses from people who don't pay child support. Did not pass.

**FOR MORE INFORMATION:** Minnesota Women's Consortium, 550 Rice St., St. Paul, MN 55103. (612) 228-0338. *Great materials, membership is $25/year.*

## MISSISSIPPI

**1. Women's Health.** House Bill 352 and Senate Bill 2288 would have required insurance companies to pay for mammograms. Died.

**2. Family Leave.** House Bill 726 would have allowed state employees to use sick leave to care for sick children. Died.

**3. Right to Choose.** House Bill 619 would prohibit an abortion facility from operating within 1,500 feet of a church. In House Committee.

**FOR MORE INFORMATION:** League of Women Voters of Mississippi, P.O. Box 55505, Jackson, MS 39296-5505. (601) 352-4616. *Newsletter for members. Legislative information: (601) 359-3217.*

## MISSOURI

**1. Right to Choose.** House Bill 1048 would have outlawed abortion but died in committee. House Bill 1714 would require a woman seeking an abortion to visit a state-sanctioned pregnancy counselor who advocates carrying the pregnancy to term. Not likely to pass.

**2. Women's Health.** House Bill 1558 would allocate money for early cervical cancer testing, pap smears and mammograms. Dead for this year.

**3. Clinic Access.** Senate Bill 603 and House Bill 1508 would make it illegal to prevent someone from entering/leaving a medical facility by physically detaining them or obstructing passage. Status: Likely to be delayed.

**FOR MORE INFORMATION:** Planned Parenthood Affiliates of Missouri, P.O. Box 395, Jefferson City, MO 65102. (314) 634-2761. *Free legislative updates and information sheets on family planning, women's health.*

**Minnesota is the first state to have a majority of women serving on its Supreme Court.**

# MONTANA

*The Montana legislature only meets in odd-numbered years.On the 1993 agenda:*
**1. Right to Choose.** Anti-choice forces bombed the Planned Parenthood clinic in Helena (the only one in the state). As a result, legislation to curb clinic violence is expected to be introduced in 1993.
**2. Women and Social Services.** Montana is having a budget crisis; funding for services like child care and family planning has been drastically cut. Lobbyists are pushing for tax reforms to generate funding for these services.
**FOR MORE INFORMATION:** Montana Women's Lobby, P.O. Box 1099, Helena, MT 59624. (406) 449-7917. *Quarterly newsletters and biweekly legislative reports available for $25/year.*

# NEBRASKA

**1. Right to Choose.** Legislative Bill 78 would have delayed abortions 24 hours, required patients to learn about the physiological characteristics of the fetus. Died.
**2. Health Care.** Legislative Bill 1077 would have eliminated funding for medical assistance to pregnant women on Aid to Families with Dependent Children (AFDC). Died.
**3. Family Leave.** Legislative Bill 145 would have required businesses with 100+ employees (2% of all companies in the state) to provide workers with 6 weeks of unpaid, job-protected leave. Died.
**FOR MORE INFORMATION:** NOW-Omaha Chapter, P.O. Box 3325, Omaha, NE 68108. (402) 556-4793. *Newsletter for members.*

# NEVADA

*The Nevada legislature only meets in odd-numbered years. On the 1993 agenda:*
**1. Family Leave.** A 1991 family leave bill that had been too watered down for supporters will be revamped and reintroduced.
**2. Low-Income Women.** Welfare is a big issue—lobbyists are working to get legislation drafted that would make more money available for Aid to Families with Dependent Children (AFDC).
**3. Right to Choose.** In 1990, *Roe v. Wade* was codified (made state law) by a public vote. In 1993, anti-choice factions will try to pass a parental consent bill.
**FOR MORE INFORMATION:** Nevada Women's Political Caucus, P.O. Box 172, Genoa, NV 89411. (702) 782-3067. *Free quarterly newsletter.*

**The average female college graduate earns less than the average male high school graduate.**

# NEW HAMPSHIRE

**1. Right to Choose.** House Bill 1407 would repeal pre-*Roe v.Wade* laws that criminalize abortion. Also up: A parental notification bill (Senate Bill 456) sponsored by Senator Humphrey. Passed, but governor vetoed.

**2. Women's Health.** Some insurance companies don't cover a breast cancer treatment called *autologous bone marrow transplant* (ABMT)—recognized by the American Cancer Society—but cover treatments for other cancers. Senate Bill 363 would require companies to cover ABMT. Passed in both houses, awaiting governor's signature.

**3. Sexual Assault.** Senate Bill 472-FN would set tougher penalties for convicted rapists and clarify the definition of sexual assault. Awaiting governor's signature.

**FOR MORE INFORMATION:** New Hampshire Women's Lobby, P.O. Box 1072, Concord, NH 03302-1072. (603) 224-9105. *Membership is $25/ year, includes legislative updates and newsletter.*

# NEW JERSEY

**1. Right to Choose.** Assembly Bill 565 would require parental notification before a minor's abortion; judicial bypass would only be an option with proven abuse in the home. Status: Passage possible.

**2. Sexual Harassment.** Senate Bill 85 would revise the current civil rights law by defining and recognizing sexual harassment in places other than the workplace. Status: In Senate Judiciary Committee, passage uncertain.

**3. Stalking.** Senate Bill 256 would criminalize willful and/or repeated incidences of following and harassing someone. In Senate Judiciary Committee.

**FOR MORE INFORMATION:** National Organization for Women— New Jersey Chapter, 114 West State Street, Trenton, NJ 08608. (609) 393-0156. *Quarterly newsletter for members.*

# NEW MEXICO

**1. Right to Choose.** In 1991 a bill was introduced to require women to get a state-sanctioned lecture and wait 24 hours before an abortion. Tabled, will be back in 1993.

**2. Domestic Violence.** Senate Bill 27 would provide funding for a statewide resource and referral center for domestic violence. Status: Tabled in Senate Finance Committee—will be back in 1993.

The average female high school graduate earns less than the average male high school dropout.

**3. Women's Health.** House Bill 223 would require insurance companies to cover Pap smears and mammograms. Passed in the House and Senate, awaiting the governor's signature.

**FOR MORE INFORMATION:** NOW-New Mexico, P.O. Box 137-B, 2801 Rodeo Rd., Sante Fe, NM 87505. (505) 989-6639. *Newsletter for members.*

# NEW YORK

**1. Women's Health.** Family planning funding is at 1991 levels but the governor is proposing to slash funds for programs ranging from prenatal care outreach to breast cancer detection.

**2. Right to Choose.** Senate Bill 5182/Assembly Bill 10750 would require physicians to notify both parents before minors can get abortions, with few exceptions. Sponsors: Senator Padavan and Assembly Member Dearie. Status: The Assembly is pro-choice, little chance for passage.

• Senate Bills 6000A and 6026 would have ended New York's long-standing policy of providing Medicaid funding for abortions. Dead.

**FOR MORE INFORMATION:** Family Planning Advocates of New York State, 17 Elk Street, Abany, NY 12207-1002. (518) 436-8408. *Free legislative updates for members. Call or write for information.*
• New York State Division for Women, Executive Chamber, State Capitol, Albany, NY 12224. (518) 474-3612.

# NORTH CAROLINA

**1. Family Leave.** House Bill 930 would require companies with 25+ employees to give workers up to 12 weeks of unpaid leave to take care of children. Status: Passage unlikely this session.

**2. Right to Choose.** Senate Bill 318 would require a minor to get one parent's consent in order to get an abortion. Status: Tabled; will probably be back.

**3. Women and Labor Laws.** Since the Imperial Foods fire in Hamlet, which killed 25 workers (mostly black women), lobbyists are pushing for labor law reforms. Status: No legislation introduced yet.

**FOR MORE INFORMATION:** NC Equity Women's Agenda Program, 505 Oberlin Road, Raleigh, NC 27605. (800) 451-8065, ext. 31. Outside North Carolina: (919) 833-4055. *Free newsletters and legislative updates.*

In N.C., women head 98% of families receiving Aid to Families with Dependent Children (AFDC

# NORTH DAKOTA

*Note: The North Dakota legislature meets in odd-numbered years. 1993 preview:*

**1. Domestic Violence.** Since 1990, domestic violence has increased 70% in North Dakota. Lobbyists plan to introduce anti-domestic violence legislation that includes an anti-stalking bill.

**2. Clinic Access.** Women have been harassed at Fargo Women's Health Organization, the state's only abortion clinic. Activists hope to introduce a bill that would outlaw clinic harassment.

**3. Right to Choose.** In 1991, legislation passed (House Bill 1515) outlawing abortion in most cases—but Governor Skinner vetoed it. House Bill 1579—requiring women to hear a state-sanctioned lecture and wait 24 hours before an abortion—became law. However, Fargo is contesting the law's constitutionality.

**FOR MORE INFORMATION:** North Dakota Women's Political Caucus, 2701 North Elm, Fargo, ND 58102. *Newsletter for members.*

# OHIO

**1. Right to Choose.** House Bill 108, requiring a 24-hour wait and a state-mandated lecture before an abortion, passed in 1991. However, the ACLU has challenged its constitutionality and it is not being enforced.

**2. Family Leave.** House Bill 424 would require companies with 50+ employees to provide workers up to 8 weeks of job-protected, unpaid leave. Status: In Rules Committee; could go either way.

**3. Women's Health.** House Bill 142 will require insurance companies to pay for mammograms. Passed, effective July 1, 1992.

**FOR MORE INFORMATION:** Women's Policy and Research Commission, 30 East Broad Street, B-1 Level, Columbus, OH 43266. (614) 466-5580 or (800) 282-3040 (in Ohio only). *Write for a free publications list.*

# OKLAHOMA

**1. Right to Choose.** House Bill 1951 would have prohibited abortions except when the life of the mother was in danger; defeated.

• Three parental notification bills (House Bills 2028, 2034 and 2276) were filed this year. House Bill 2028 is awaiting a vote, passage is likely.

• In September 1990, an initiative petition was filed to outlaw abortion. It's been challenged in the Supreme Court; pro-choice forces suspect foul play involving the signatures. The issue will likely appear on the November ballot. Passage likely.

**Since 1969, the number of women state legislators has more than quadrupled.**

**2. Stalking.** House Bill 2291 would criminalize the act of maliciously and/or repeatedly following or harassing a person. Status: In Senate Committee.

**FOR MORE INFORMATION:** Oklahoma Women's Network, P.O. Box 14339, Tulsa, OK 74159-1339. (918) 744-0303. *Newsletter for members.*

# OREGON

*The Oregon legislature meets in odd-numbered years. Recent highlights and upcoming legislation:*

**1. Family Leave.** In 1991 a bill was passed requiring companies with 35+ employees to give workers up to 12 weeks of unpaid, job-protected leave.

**2. Sex Discrimination.** Legislation will be introduced in 1993 that would allow victims of sex discrimination in the workplace to collect punitive damages. The most victims can now get is job restitution and back pay.

**3. Clinic Access.** In 1991 a bill was passed making it illegal to obstruct or impede an individual's access to a medical facility.

**FOR MORE INFORMATION:** Oregon Women's Political Caucus, P.O. Box 40465, Portland, OR 97240. (503) 224-2588. *Newsletters and legislative updates for members.*

# PENNSYLVANIA

**1. Family Leave.** Senate Bill 529 would allow employees more time off for family leave than the national family leave bill. Status: In Committee.

**2. Right to Choose.** Senate Bill 1392, introduced by Senator Schwartz, would repeal sections of the 1989 Abortion Control Act. Passage unlikely.

**3. Gender Balance.** House Bill 1286, sponsored by Rep. Rudy, would require an equal number of women and men appointees to state boards and commissions by 1996. Status: In House State Government Committee.

**FOR MORE INFORMATION:** NOW for Pennsylvania, P.O. Box 17326, Pittsburgh, PA 15235. (412) 795-3972.

# RHODE ISLAND

**1. Right to Choose.** Four pro-choice bills have been filed; the most significant (House Bill 7549) would codify *Roe v. Wade* (keep the right to choose legal in the state). Status: In the House awaiting a vote.

**2. Family Leave.** House Bill 7864 would amend the current family leave law so that businesses with 20+ employees (as opposed to 50+) would be

Twenty-two states have introduced or plan to introduce legislation calling for

required to give workers 13 weeks of unpaid, job-protected leave. In Labor Committee; no hearing scheduled. Passage uncertain.

**FOR MORE INFORMATION:** Rhode Island Choice Coalition, P.O. Box 28678, Providence, RI 02908. (401) 421-7820. *What's available: State representatives' voting records, tips on assessing candidates.*

## SOUTH CAROLINA

**1. Women's Health.** Senate Bill 1148, House Bill 4236 would require insurance companies to pay for Pap smears and mammograms. In Committee.

**2. Right to Choose.** Under House Bill 3866, women would have to hear an anti-abortion lecture before an abortion. In House Judiciary Committe.

**3. Clinic Access.** House Bill 3189 would make it illegal to prevent someone from entering/leaving a medical facility. In House Judiciary Committee.

**FOR MORE INFORMATION:** South Carolina Women's Consortium, P.O. Box 3099, Columbia, SC 29230. (803) 252-9813. *Monthly newsletter that includes legislative updates available for $15/year.*

## SOUTH DAKOTA

**1. Stalking.** Senate Bill 157 would make it illegal to follow or harass a person with the intention of harming them. Status: Passage likely.

**2. Right to Choose.** House Bill 1212 would mandate that schools teach chastity and sexual abstinence. Passage unlikely.

**3. Family Leave.** House Bill 1332 has been so watered down (it requires companies to give workers only two weeks' leave) that supporters have decided to reintroduce a stronger bill next session.

**FOR MORE INFORMATION:** South Dakota NARAL, 4320 South Louise Ave., Suite 103, Sioux Falls, SD 57106-3133. (605) 361-5014. *Free legislative alerts and fact sheets.*

## TENNESSEE

**1. Right to Choose.** A handful of bills to outlaw abortion are up; none are likely to pass. House Bill 1860 would require the state to pay for Norplant birth control devices for women on Aid to Families with Dependent Children (AFDC), offer $500 as an incentive to use the device. Passage unlikely.

**2. Gender Balance.** In 1991, Governor McWherter appointed an all-male board to the University of Tennessee even though the school requires that

equal numbers of women and men on state boards and commissions.

at least one woman be included. Lobbyists have drafted a law that would make information about board appointments accessible to the public.

**FOR MORE INFORMATION:** Tennessee Women's Political Caucus, P.O. Box 25211, Nashville, TN 37202. *Newsletter available for members.*

# TEXAS

*Note: The Texas legislature meets in odd-numbered years—no 1992 session. Recent highlights and upcoming legislation:*

**1. Child Care.** Several bills passed in 1991, including House Bill 1083, which will make liability insurance for child care providers more accessible and affordable. Rep. Linebarger plans to introduce more legislation.

**2. Women and Social Services.** Texas's enormous deficit has crippled the state government, and legislators are addressing it in a special session this summer. There's talk of revamping the state tax system and slashing funding for family planning, child care and social services.

**FOR MORE INFORMATION:** Texas Family Planning Association, P.O. Box 3868, Austin, TX 78764. (512) 448-4857. *Free quarterly newsletter.*

# UTAH

**1. Stalking.** House Bill 346 was introduced to protect individuals from being repeatedly followed and harassed. Passed House, in Senate Committee.

**2. Gender Balance.** Senate Bill 92 would require the governor to "strongly consider appointing persons of the underrepresented gender on commissions and boards." Passage likely.

**3. Family Leave.** Senate Bill 37 would require employers to provide workers with 4 hours of unpaid leave a year for "crisis intervention" (i.e., emergency parent-teacher conferences at their child's school). Passage unlikely.

**FOR MORE INFORMATION:** Utahns for Choice, 515 South 400 East, Suite 307, Salt Lake City, UT 84111. (801) 328-8939. *Free brochure, list of how state legislators voted on a bill to restrict abortion, voter registration forms.*

# VERMONT

**1. Family Leave.** Senate Bill 134 would require companies with 10+ employees to provide workers with 12 weeks of unpaid leave. Passed Senate.

**2. Domestic Violence.** House Bill 462 would broaden the definition of domestic violence to include abuse of all household members and people who live together. In House Judiciary Committee. Budget cuts threaten 16 domestic violence and sexual assault programs.

**3. Right to Choose.** House Bill 490 would require parental notification for minors' abortions. H 386 would institute a 24-hour wait, require women to hear a state-sanctioned lecture before an abortion. Neither likely to pass.

**FOR MORE INFORMATION:** National Organization for Women— VT, 21 Church St., Burlington, VT 05401. *Newsletters, legislative alerts for members.*

# VIRGINIA

**1. Stalking.** House Bill 1077 would allow for prosecution of people who follow and harass someone, even if no bodily harm occurs. Status: Passed both houses, awaiting governor's signature.

**2. Clinic Access.** House Bill 1054 would forbid an individual from blocking or impeding an entrance to a medical facility. In Senate Justice Committee.

**3. Right to Choose.** House Bill 1110—requiring a minor to notify one parent before getting an abortion—was passed. Awaiting governor's signature.

**FOR MORE INFORMATION:** Virginia Women's Political Caucus, 904 Post Oak Court, Virginia Beach, VA 23464. *Materials for members.*

# WASHINGTON

**1. Right to Choose.** House Bill 2909 would have required women who have given birth to children with fetal alcohol syndrome to be fitted with the Norplant birth control device. Died.

**2. Family Leave.** House Bill 2220 would have expanded the current law to require companies with 50+ employees (it's now 100+) to give workers unpaid, job-protected leave. Passed House, died in Senate.

**3. Sexual Harassment.** House Bill 2264 would have made it easier for sexual harassment victims to collect punitive damages. Died.

**FOR MORE INFORMATION:** Washington Women United, P.O. Box 2174, Olympia, WA 98507. (206) 754-9880. *Bimonthly newsletter, legislative updates for members.*

# WEST VIRGINIA

**1. Domestic Violence.** Senate Bill 303 would allow for the arrest of a suspect without a warrant if an individual is in danger. Would also clarify and broaden the definition of domestic violence. In Senate Judiciary Committee.

**First woman nominated for president by a major political party: Margaret Chase Smith (1964).**

**2. Right to Choose.** Senate Bill 112 and House Bill 2132 would eliminate Medicaid funding for abortions. Status: Both in Committee.

• Two bills would restrict abortion: Senate Bill 194 is a parental consent law—judicial bypass would be permitted only if a teen is a victim of reported rape or incest. Senate Bill 313 would require a 24-hour wait and hearing a state-sanctioned lecture before abortions. Passage unlikely.

**FOR MORE INFORMATION:** National Organization for Women— Charleston Chapter, Attn. Sandy Fisher, Arlington Court #12, Charleston, WV 25301. *Newsletter for members.*

# WISCONSIN

**1. Right to Choose.** Assembly Bill 180 would prohibit a minor from getting an abortion without "family involvement," judicial/clergy bypass. Status: Awaiting the governor's signature.

**2. Family Leave.** Senate Bill 98 would have expanded the current family leave law by requiring companies with 35+ employees (it's now 50+) to grant workers 6 weeks of unpaid, job-protected leave. No vote, died.

**3. Sexual Harassment.** Senate Bill 1 would have amended the current civil rights law to make it possible for victims of sexual harassment to collect punitive damages. Died.

**FOR MORE INFORMATION:** Wisconsin Women's Network, 122 State St, Room 406, Madison, WI 53703. (608) 255-9809. *Free newsletter for members.*

# WYOMING

**1. Health Care.** House Bill 53 was a comprehensive health care bill that, among other things, would have established a program to help low-income women pay back doctors for medical services. Died.

**2. Women's Businesses.** Senate Files 22 would fund the development of a program to help small businesses provide employee insurance (many small businesses are owned by women). Passed in the House, died in the Senate.

**3. Sex Discrimination.** House Bill 41 would repeal certain medical test requirements in order for women to get marriage licenses (only women must get the tests). Status: Will be introduced in 1993.

**FOR MORE INFORMATION:** Wyoming Commission for Women, Herschler Building, 122 West 25th Street, Cheyenne, WY 82002. (307) 777-7349. *Free brochures and pamphlets.* After May 31: Call the Division of Labor Standards at (307) 777-7261.

**About a third of all governments in the world have no women members.**

# ELECTION RESOURCES

*A sampling of groups that deal with women and politics—from providing facts about women voters and congressional voting records to generating funds for women candidates.*

**American Association of University Women,** 1111 16th St. NW, Washington, D.C. 20036-4873. (202) 785-7737. *Has a free brochure called* Our Rights...Nothing Less: Put Your Votes Where Your Rights Are. *To order, call (800) 225-9998 or write: AAUW Sales Office, P.O. Box 2012, Annapolis Junction, MD 20701-2012.*

**Business and Professional Women/USA,** 2012 Massachusetts Ave. NW, Washington D.C. 20036. (202) 293-1100. *National membership ($55-$85 a year, depending on the state)organization with local chapters. Has a variety of resources, including congressional voting charts.*

**Center for the American Woman and Politics,** Eagleton Institute of Politics, Rutgers University, New Brunswick, NJ 08901. (908) 828-2210. *Has done extensive research on women elected and appointed to office. Call or write for publications list, free fact sheets.*

**Congressional Caucus for Women's Issues,** 2471 Rayburn Bldg., Washington, D.C. 20515. (202) 225-6740. *A legislative service organization of 170 members of Congress that's dedicated to promoting women's legal and economic rights. Free fact sheets on topics like women's health, pay equity and sexual harassment.*

**EMILY's List,** 1112 16th St. NW, Suite 750, Washington, D.C. 20036. (202) 887-1957. *Raises money for pro-choice Democratic women candidates. Write or call for details.*

**Fund for the Feminist Majority,** 1600 Wilson Blvd., Suite 704, Arlington, VA 22209. (703) 522-2214. *Sponsors campaigns on everything from organizing pro-choice marches to encouraging women to run for office. Has a booklet called "The Feminization of Power,"an in-depth look at feminist campaign strategies. Cost: $5.*

**League of Women Voters,** 1730 M St. NW, Washington, D.C. 20036. (202) 429-1965. *A nonpartisan organization that provides general information on assessing candidates. What's available:*

An estimated 68% of American women are registered to vote (compared to 65% of men).

The Women's Vote: Beyond the Nineteenth Amendment, *a report on gender differences in voting (Publication #425, $1.75)* and Pick a Candidate, *a brochure about assessing candidates' records (Publication #259, 35¢). Note: No phone orders.*

**Ms. magazine,** P.O. Box 57131, Boulder, CO 80322-7131. (800) 365-5232. *Not an organization, but features some of the most comprehensive women's election coverage around. Rates candidates' records on domestic issues, civil rights, right to choose, etc. Subscription: $30/year.*

**National Black Women's Political Leadership Caucus,** 3005 Bladensburg Road NE, Suite 217, Washington, D.C. 20018. (202) 529-2806. *Provides information about voter registration and the political and economic process. Hosts seminars and an annual legislative conference. Call for details.*

**National Organization for Women (NOW),** 1000 16th St. #700, Washington, D.C. 20036. (202) 331-0066. *With 250,000 members, NOW is one of the strong-arms of the women's movement. Membership is $35 and includes newsletters with legislative updates.*

**National Women's Party,** Sewall-Belmont House, 144 Constitution Ave. NE, Washington, D.C. 20002. (202) 546-1210. *A nonpartisan, nonprofit group founded in 1913 by Alice Paul, author of the Equal Rights Amendment. Passage of the ERA is still its main goal. Sliding scale membership fee of $15-$25 includes quarterly newsletter and legislative updates.*

**National Women's Political Caucus,** 1275 K St. NW, #750, Washington, D.C. 20005. (202) 898-1100. *What's available:* A Woman's Guide to the 1992 Democratic Presidential Candidates *and* A Woman's Guide to the 1992 Republican Presidential Candidates *($3.50 each),* Congress' Voting Record on Women's Issues *($2).*

**The WISH List,** 730 Columbus Ave., Suite 187, New York, NY 10025. *Raises money for Republican women candidates. Write for free brochure.*

**Women's Campaign Fund,** 120 Maryland Ave. NE, Washington, D.C. 20002. (202) 544-4484. *A bipartisan organization that supports pro-choice candidates on the federal, state, and local levels.*

Average age of first-time women candidates: mid 40s. First-time men: late 20s.